ARE YOU TALKING
TO ME?

ARE YOU TALKING TO ME?

Will Richardsson

TABLE OF CONTENTS

Udo Kier: Time is a Sin! 1
Mark Webber: Quintessential Independent 3
Josh Hartnett: Anti-Star 5
John Rhys Davies: Not Just a Pretty Face 7
Costa-Gavras: Piece de Resistance 9
In Search of Mike Tyson 14
Fun Lovin' Criminal Behavior 27
Rutger Hauer: Surfing the Blue Screen 35
Jon Lord: Smoke on the Keyboard 41
Really Being There with Phil Niblock 46
Bruce Willis: Still Lazy After All Those Years 52
Scott Schulman: A Dedicated Follower of Fashion 56
Richard Horowitz: A Unique Way of Seeing 62
Jan Kaczmarek: Soundtrack of Life 75
Gene Gutowski Does Not Need This Interview 85
Andrei Konchalovsky: Twice in a Lifetime 99
The Man in the White Suit, The Stig 106
A Few Rounds with Vladimir Klitschko 110
A Matter of Life and Breath: Aneta Kopacz, Film Director 121
The Poet of the Sandinistas 125
John Lydon: International Treasure 129

Introduction

Ladies and Gentlemen, let me introduce you to a book whose words are arranged unlike any other that you will ever read. Indeed, unique! This little book contains wisdom, passion, and enough exclamation points for the ages. It is a series of interviews with some of the most talented individuals you are ever likely not to meet, especially if you're like my British cousin who moans, "I never met anyone famous, except for the Queen." Indeed. These people have made a name for themselves with their skills, talents, and personalities. To me, these are timeless testaments to the struggle to be original.

Now, I know what you're thinking, "Hey Will, how can a mere book about virtuosi in their fields be that interesting in this age of instant information and readers with the attention span of an Adderall freak surfing Tiktok? How the heck would I know? Nonetheless, these individuals are not just top talents with captivating stories. They're also funny, quirky, and sometimes even a little bit nutty. Raise your hand, Mike Tyson, who cheerfully asked me at the end of our interview, "Do you know where I can get some weed?" His knowledge of F. Scott Fitzgerald and his interest in Polish history shocked me.

What else? You'll meet athletes who can lick their weight in wildcats like Vladimir Klitschko, painstaking artists like Phil Niblock who can produce an original masterpiece out of the most ordinary material, and musicians who can build a tune that will make you jump up and down like granny at a hootenanny. Between these pages, John Lord's My Woman from Tokyo enjoys a little anarchy in the UK. Thank you, Mr. Lydon. And, best of all, you'll hear about their lives, struggles (including how to die hard with Mr. Willis), triumphs, often unbelievable adventures, and their commitment to excellence, all in their own words.

Just sit back, relax, and let your mind's eye transport you to another realm - twenty different ones. This book is like a backstage pass to the world of talent, where the only thing that matters is what you can do and how you do it.

If you're looking for a book that will inspire you, make you laugh, provoke both daydreams and nightmares, and maybe even make you slightly envious, then you might find a home between these pages. There is always that chance. Anyway, I had a whale of a time doing the interviews. Because these interviews are not just about gifted and notable personages, they're about people and how in their particular circumstances, they've used their particular talents to carve their niche in the world. Influential they are and not an "influencer" amongst them.

Oh yes, all of these interviews took place in the 2010s in Warsaw, Poland, either in person or using the internet. Most were published in Malemen magazine, a now-defunct organ. Tyson, Klitschko, and Gutowski were cover stories. Since the interviews were conducted, Jon, Gene, and Rutger have passed on. Bruce Willis has dementia (He told me he was living the dream and is now descending into one. Aren't we all?) Andrei Konchalovsky's summation of the Asia-gazing-gangster tendency of the Russian leadership proved to be Nostradamus-like. The Russian director, Andrei, and the Ukrainian boxer, Vladimir, are trapped on opposing sides of the most harrowing conflict since WWII. And since interviewing Aneta about her cancer documentary film, I made one of my own about an immunologist searching for a cancer cure. At almost the same time, several of my close colleagues contracted cancer. Three: Ade, Artur, and Luke died. One, Elisabeth, survived.

So, go ahead and make my day. You can order this paperback on Amazon Kindle and judge if the kind of talent that inspired all these personalities to tell these stories was worth the hullabaloo. I'm betting that you will find that it was. Unfortunately, the last time I won a bet was with Winston Carlisle over who would take Kathy Doverspike to the high school prom. Winston won, and I collected. It's a sumptuous and, one hopes, satisfying meal cooked with the ingredients these impressively unique individuals provided.

WRR, Warsaw, February, 2023

Udo Kier: Time is a Sin!

U do and I are killing time in the Off Camera VIP café. Not literally. But we wish we could kill time because Time with a capital T is a bastard. Nobody knows that more that Udo Kier, who was once so beautiful he made mouths water like a bell does for one of Pavlov's dogs.

Udo early on was a master of the monster movie, one of the most well-known character actors in movies. His face is unforgettable. He's worked with Fassbinder and Madonna, Von Trier and Pamela Anderson, Gus van Sant and Scooby Doo.

His latest film, the sci-fi spoof, Iron Sky, is vintage Udo: he leads a Nazi mission to colonize the moon in 1945. Udo of course has played his share of villains, starting with Dr. Frankenstein in Flesh for Frankenstein (1973), his big break. The film's director, Paul Morrissey, sat next to Udo on a plane flight from Rome to Munich.

Need I say more? I mean, bring it on. Bring it on.

Now Udo lives in Palm Springs, California, where at 68 years old he is still a relative Spring Chicken. The actor who was the most beautiful man in the world hates getting old. He works more now than ever.

"In the restaurant, they say pass the salt please young man," he laughs.

He bought and renovated a library in town and owns a ranch not far away. He has his own well and solar heating at the ranch.

"I live in the desert so I can live in the light. Actors like to be in the light."

Udo! The surname is an unnecessary formality. The face is one of the most recognized in cinema.

He's made over 200 European and American films.

He has channelled vampires from the Polanski-produced Blood for

Dracula (1974) to more recent fang-films like Blade, Modern Vampires Shadow and Dracula 300.

WRR: It's hard for me to talk to you, Udo, without your Hollywood entourage stopping our conversation. Can you take care of that?

UK: I can arrange some people to annoy you.

WRR: Thanks. I'd like that. I'd feel more like I'm in LA. But seriously, what's it like living in the desert.

UK: Hot, hot, hot!

WRR: Nice one. So how do you pass the time?

UK: Time is a sin!

WRR: Spoken like a true Dracula!

UK: Past 60, you want to spend your time carefully... So, time is important... But I'm glad to be here because I wanted to spend some time in Poland. I never have. I love the square (in Krakow). Wonderful!

WRR: Tell me some Warhol stories, please.

UK: When we were filming Frankenstein in Rome ($300,000/3 weeks/ in 3D), Andy was there to do interviews. He was extremely popular in Italy and Germany then. Andy always had four or five people with him and a tape recorder like you have now, but bigger...He would speak very softly and the rest of us were speaking loudly, so we would all be on the tape...His secretary would type it up and this went into the diary of Andy Warhol... He always wore blue jeans. He wore awfully expensive jackets and beautiful shoes, but he always wore blue jeans. And he always had a plastic bag which had the big Polaroid camera in it. He took these instant pictures all the time...

WRR: Did he give you any special artwork?

UK: Sure. Oh, I have so many things from him that say for Udo with love. For example, there was an issue of Interview (Warhol's celebrated magazine) with Polanski on the cover. And Polanski had said something nice about me in the article.

WRR: What did he say?

UK: I can't tell you. I don't remember exactly. So, if you don't do something exactly then I don't do it. I'm not an inventor. I tell the truth... So, I said to Andy, can you sign the magazine for me. And he said, where? And I said every page. So, I have the magazine and he signed every page. There's about forty or fifty pages.

WRR: So, you could sell each page.

UK: Good idea! I will do that when I get older and need money. Nie ma problema.

Mark Webber: Quintessential Independent

Mark Webber is independent from head to toe. He sees the system; He uses the system. He suffers from no Josh-style angst, and he is having the time of his life now making the indie films Hartnett might envy.

He's not only written, directed and acted, but raised the budget of his last film through a friend, a Vegan ice cream shop owner in LA. (I'm not making this up).

Fresh from a reasonable showing at Sundance, accompanied by his new girlfriend Teresa Palmer, the young Australian star, Mark Webber was in Krakow with his film The End of Love. Respectably reviewed in The Hollywood Reporter, Mark had his eye on the $100,000 grand prize from the Off Camera festival.

WRR: "I have not prepared as well for this interview as I did for Costa-Gavras for the simple reason that I didn't know until yesterday that I would have the pleasure.

MW: That's fine! Don't worry

WRR: But I did happen to find and watch—wait for it—Snow Day (2000) last night. (Snow Day was a remarkably successful studio formula comedy that got Webber noticed both in Hollywood and by a larger public.)

MW: Oh, my fucking god. Of all the films!

WRR: I know, I know. But I enjoyed it.

MW: That's hilarious!

WRR: Chevy Chase, Pam Grier... Iggy Pop. What was it like working with him?

MW: He was great. But at the time it was funny. I had to research who Iggy Pop was. I was like 19 years old, and I never really listened to his music. It wasn't till later that I realized Fuck I did a movie with Iggy Pop.

WRR: What was he like?

MW: He was just a regular guy. Funny and sweet. Charming and so not like a punk rock god! He took it very seriously.

WRR: He's a pro's pro.

MW: Yep. He's a total pro.

WRR: He's one of the most professional people ever!

MW: I know! It's true!

WRR: So how did you start out in showbiz?

MW: All I ever wanted to do was be an actor. I had this tough up-bringing and this amazing mother who taught me that I could be anything I wanted to be. (His mother is noted homeless advocate Cheri Honkala, who was the Green Party candidate for vice-president in 2012.) I never really had any doubt about being an actor. I was young and fearless in a way. I was very passionate about making films. Still am. I got lucky with my mom. Navigating though Hollywood, it's been really great being grounded in reality.

WRR: Tell me about The End of Love.

MW: It's my second film. I made it with my son, who was two at the time. In it I'm obsessed with realism. I've always approached every film I've been in to make it as natural as possible. I thought I haven't really seen a film about a father and son with a struggling single father. I got the idea to build the film around my son's life, his moods, his rhythms.

WRR: And you've had a good reception.

MW: Yes, people have been kind. It has sold well. It's been a huge accomplishment for me.

Josh Hartnett: Anti-Star

Whatever happened to Josh Hartnett? It's been a common question in Hollywood for several years.

In Krakow we are asking the same thing. He's 30 minutes late for the press conference. Somebody tells me: "I heard him say yesterday that he doesn't have anything interesting to say."

My YouTube surfing of his earlier interviews shows rather the opposite, an articulate and thoughtful actor who feels betrayed by his good looks that often hover on the borderline between stunning and geeky.

Finally, he ambles in, that famously symmetrical face bisected by a shy, forgive-me smile.

"I'm sorry but we went for a tour of the salt mines, and it took longer than we thought," he says, a regular guy who just happens to be a star.

Hartnett has famously hated his stardom. It's an industry cliché. In person he is much bigger than you think. Most actors are usually much smaller. That is a surprise. The Minnesota native is a modern Gary Cooper. He is the same height and weight as the great Coop (1.9m and 85 kilos). In a former age he would have been an obvious cowboy star. Don't laugh. Steve McQueen, Clint Eastwood, Lee Marvin, John Wayne, Jimmy Stewart, Coop, all found fame in horse operas.

JH is perhaps the most puzzling of all stars in his age-range. He's graced more magazine covers than Hugh Grant in his heyday. Get this: he turned down the Christopher Reeve inheritance: the Superman franchise. (The original 1950s TV superman, George Reeves, committed suicide.) He turned down a $100 million three picture deal as the Man of Steel. This is independence of an incredibly special variety.

"Independence means the ability to choose," he says. "Hollywood has a lot to offer. Certain actors and directors have achieved independence."

5

Is he his own worst enemy, too independent for his own good? Maybe. He certainly laid his career on the line in about 2005 and stomped the shit out of it. By his own admission he has turned down a number of excellent projects. Superman would have given him super freedom to produce and direct, which is what he says he wants to do.

"This is a director's medium," he says. Fellini was his first favourite film director. He wants to work with Lars von Trier.

His somewhat wacky career, full of capricious choices and the unfortunate foregoing of plum roles in favour of some, seems a waste of a surprisingly robust talent. The very system he is rebelling against would seem to showcase him in the best light. He is a natural leading man in the classic sense. At his best he is one of the most watchable actors in cinema. See Black Hawk Down, Sin City (he opens and closes the film), parts of Lucky Number Slevin, 30 Days of Night (a rather good vampire movie). And Mozart and the Whale, in which he plays a victim of Asperger's Syndrome. That's a good little independent film. On the other hand, Bunraku, the martial arts action film he made in 2008, is yet another strange choice.

Look, here's the thing. Any film that makes it through development and hits a reasonable number of screens is a small miracle. As William Goldman, the great screenwriter, famously said, when it comes to knowing at the start whether a film will be good or not, "nobody knows."

So, it's not so surprising to hear Hartnett say, "I've turned down a lot of good films. I don't always make good choices. Here's a guess: better, tougher choices are ahead.

John Rhys Davies: Not Just a Pretty Face

I'm saying, "Do you think you were typecast as Gimli in Lord of the Rings? Was there something so dwarf like about you that you were the obvious choice for the role?"

John Rhys-Davies throws a left hook.

I bend my knees and throw an uppercut to his chin that lifts him out of his shoes.

"Take that you freakin' midget!"

* * *

Just kidding.

We are standing in the VIP bar doing Richard Burton impressions. My baritone vs. JRD's basso profundo. Richard Burton was a famous Welsh actor of stage and screen who was once married to Elizabeth Taylor and who drank himself to death. "When I was hewing the dark womb of the earth," says John in imitation Burton. "To be or not to be," say I.

Switching to southern accents now.

"Is that sugah?" says John. Anna, my gorgeous pouting assistant, has offered him sugar for his coffee.

"Yep. It sure does look like it, honey chile," I say (hungover Rhett Butler accent.)

"Do I look like I need some sweetening up?" he says.

This is his first time in Poland in many years.

"We are all friends of Poland," says John. "The Polish pilots in the Battle of Britain did more than their share to save us. It's a matter of great hurt to me that we went into the war to defend Poland and ended up abandoning it to the Russians."

"Yalta."

"An Iron Curtain has descended over Europe," John does his best Churchill.

There is something refreshingly old school about JRD, something pleasingly avuncular. He is no amateur in life or in work. A theatre man who went into movies, which is the typical British transition. From the Royal Shakespeare Company (1970s) to Sallah in Indiana Jones (1980s) to Professor Arturo in Sliders 1990s) to world renown in the Lord of the Rings (2000s), each decade he has grown into bigger roles from high-brow British theatre to mass-market blockbusters.

"Being creative is so difficult. It's hard to let go. You think: I didn't quite get that right, but one of the things that any creative person must do is to learn to let go. Sometimes you just have to let go and move on. There are times you cannot rework and rework," he says.

He thrives on transition. Despite growing up in Africa, his working-class background made him radical leftist in the '60s, that is, until he heard a young Margaret Thatcher speak. He went to heckle and ended up falling under her spell. She was as great speaker even then, he says. He bucks the Hollywood trend. He's a political conservative who risked his career speaking his mind about growing Muslim population and fundamentalism in Europe and the resulting demographic changes it suggests.

A family man, he stuck with his first wife until she lost her battle with Alzheimer's. He once tracked down and rescued his war-photographer son in Croatia. He now lives in Hollywood and on the Isle of Man with his second wife and has a six-year-old daughter who is "the love of my life."

* * *

Outside in the market square, Marta Wojtal is rapidly firing her camera at John. People recognize him. Autographs are requested.

"It's a tough job but someone has to do it," says John, who adds he tries to live everyday as if it's going to be his last. Why?

"You never know when it will be." I'll drink to that.

Which reminds me of my favourite Gimli quote: "Certainty of death? Small chance of success.

What are we waiting for?"

Costa-Gavras: Piece de Resistance

I had watched Z again a couple of days before in preparation for meeting its director. And the movie was every bit as good as I remembered.

Z remains in the first rank of political melodramas. It's the proto-type of the fast-paced thriller that marries political relevance with audience-pleasing pace.

To date, it has been often copied but never surpassed. See The French Connection, The Conversation and The Day of the Jackal. Z encapsulated the spirit of the times, the late 60s, but it remains refreshingly apt today.

It was Paris-based Costa-Gavras' response to Greek dictatorship and it introduced the director's signature method of mixing incisive political commentary with his own seductive dramatic concoction. An incorruptible judge investigates the killing of a reformist politician, played by Yves Montand. As democracy disappears in a fog of conspiracy and cover-up, the film becomes a critique of the US-backed coup in Greece and the military junta of 1967-74. The film takes no prisoners in taking Greek fascism to task. Sly wit makes you roll your eyes with the credits as you watch a list of things banned by the moronic Regime of the Colonels, as the Junta was known.

The things banned by the Greek Junta included peace movements, strikes, labour unions, long hair on men, The Beatles, Sophocles, Tolstoy, Aeschylus, any mention that Socrates might be homosexual, Ionesco, Sartre, Anton Chekhov, Pinter, Edward Albee, Mark Twain, Samuel Beckett(who won the 1969 Nobel Prize for Literature), Trotsky, sociology, encyclopaedias, free press, and new math. The letter Z was banned, too. Z was used as a symbolic reminder that the assassinated senator, Grigoris Lambrakis, whose murder is the film's foundation, and the spirit of resistance he embodied, live on, notwithstanding the most nefarious efforts of the Junta. Zi = He lives.

It is an amazing list that exposes the stultifying paranoia of reactionary forces both Right and Left. Extremism is always the enemy in politics. Oppression came in two flavours: fascism and communism, both flavoured with suspicion and bathed in fear and loathing.

Z premiered in February, just in time for the Oscars. Lists were important in 1969, a year of staggering seismic movements in politics and society. It started with a Czech immolating himself and ended with the Hells Angels killing a member of the audience at Altamont. In January, Jan Palach set himself on fire in Prague to protest the Soviet invasion of Czechoslovakia. Nixon was sworn in as President of the United States. Elvis was in the studio recording Suspicious Minds (nice little irony there). The Beatles gave their last public performance on the roof of a building in London. The Godfather was published. British troops arrived to Northern Ireland. De Gaulle resigned. The Stonewall Riots mark the beginning of the Gay Rights movement in the US. The Soccer War between Honduras and El Salvador happened. The US put a man on the moon. Manson murdered. Woodstock happened. Gaddafi took power in Libya. Ho Chi Minh died. The My Lai massacre, Vietnam's most shameful incident, became public.

Z was the first film to be nominated for an Oscar as Best Picture and Best Foreign film. It won Best Foreign Films. The highly respected film critic Roger Ebert (who recently [???] died) named Z the best film of 1969 citing the screenplay and its message. He wrote: "[Z] is a film of our time. It is

about how even moral victories are corrupted. It will make you weep and will make you angry. It will tear your guts out… When the Army junta staged its coup in 1967, the right-wing generals and the police chief were cleared of all charges and "rehabilitated." Those responsible for unmasking the assassination now became political criminals. These would seem to be completely political events, but the young director Costa-Gavras has told them in a style that is almost unbearably exciting. Z is at the same time a political cry of rage and a brilliant suspense thriller. It even ends in a chase: Not through the streets but through a maze of facts, alibis and official corruption."

* * *

Costa-Gavras is waiting for me in the press room in the Pod Baran-ami palace. He is wearing a dark suit, white shirt and thick red socks.

WRR: I hope you don't mind me keeping my hat on, but I have this vicious cold. It snowed here every day for two weeks. It just stopped a week ago…

CG: Yes, the weather has been disgusting in Paris too.

WRR: How are you finding things in Krakow? You've been here before, of course.

CG: Yes, I have. I like it very much. You know the first time I came here I came from Brussels. I arrived by train. And coming out of the train I could hear people shouting, Taxi for Auschwitz! Taxi for Auschwitz! It was bizarre.

WRR: This is a good point. I call it Death Tourism. Some people seem addicted to it. Somebody asked me yesterday do I want to go to Auschwitz tomorrow, and I said, "No. I don't want to. I know what happened there."

CG: Yes, of course. But this is an amazing city. The people are nice, and the restaurants are good.

WRR: But it's not Paris. So, you've been living in Paris for how long?

CG: 60 years. I went to the Sorbonne to study comparative literature. Coming from Greece, I was a huge fan of Randolph Scott. You know him?

WRR: Yes, Westerns.

CG: So those were the movies I watched in Greece. But when I came to France I went to the cinema and the first day I saw Greed (Von Stroheim, 1924). And I thought my god you can make tragedy in a mov-ie. Before I thought movies were just action and cowboys and so on. Then I saw more and more movies and decided to go to film school.

WRR: How much did your father's political activity affect your decision to become an artist (his father was imprisoned as a suspected communist during the Greek Civil War)?

CG: The experience of my father made me run away from Greece. I escaped Greece because I thought the country was not good for people like me, from my class. In France I was amazed to see that college was for free and there were rooms for the students to stay in and the library was free. So, because of the freedom there France became my country.

WRR: What is it about France? You like it. I like it, but lots of people don't.

C-G: Yes, you are right. People say to me: how can you bear the French? What I discovered about the French was something that Jacques Prevert said. Are you familiar with him?

11

WRR: Yes. He wrote Les Paroles.

C-G: And he wrote Les Enfant du Paradis. He says in a poem: "I don't want to be the strongest, the richest, the smartest the most beautiful. I want to be different." For me France is something like this, trying to be different.

WRR: And so are you… You have chosen to make politically themed films like Z and State of Siege and Missing and Betrayed for example. Betrayed is Tom Berenger's favourite of his performances.

C-G: Yes, he was very good, and Debra Winger was excellent.

WRR: What happened to her?

C-G: Hollywood. 38, 40 years old and you are out. (See Searching for Debra Winger, the documentary).

WRR: Tant pis! You are known for making political movies that make statements. Is that an apt summation?

C-G: With a movie we don't make a political speech. We make a show. Why do we go to a show? We go to love, to hate, to feel something. That is what I'm trying to produce in my films. I'm not against the Avant Garde, but that reduces the audience to the minimum and it's important to have an audience. But I start with making movies that I like. After all, I'm the first viewer.

WRR: What do you rate as your favourite films?

C-G: I don't know. Probably one movie I'm sentimental about is Hannah K. The movie disappeared at once. It addresses the Israeli-Palestinian conflict in a way that everyone talks about it now. That the Palestinians deserve a place to live. So, I'm proud of that film.

WRR: What about your latest film Le Capita (a fast-paced, cold-blooded financial thriller)? Did the continuing financial crisis inspire you to tackle the subject?

C-G: The problem is much more complex than just The Crisis. All the politicians left and right and the European Union created these conditions. Look at what happened. There was tension with Turkey and the Germans sent submarines to Greece and the French sent planes. All those military goods were paid for on credit. It's not like Spain. That was stupid. The banks lent money to build all those apartments on the seacoast that no one wants to buy. The Greek situation is more complex.

WRR: Where did Greece go wrong?

C-G: Nobody knows. I think they are going to suffer for a while.

WRR: I lived in Nicaragua for two years. Fascinating place. What got you interested in Latin America? You made State of Siege and Missing about the Greek-like situation in Latin America in the seventies.

C-G: There's a justification for every film. After making the Confession (1970) I was looking into a story about an American advisor and ambassador in Greece during and after the Civil War (1950s). His name was Peurifoy, and he ran the country for two or three years. After this he went to Latin America (Guatemala where with the CIA, he deposed the Arbenz government). And after that he went to Asia where he was killed in an auto accident. So, I was trying to find out about this guy. Then I found out there was a whole new modern school of American advisors like CIA agent, Dan Mitrone, in Uruguay who taught torture techniques and worked with the regime police. Opposing him were the Tupamaros. They were like Robin Hoods in the beginning. No violence. Then they kidnapped him and killed him when the government refused to release political prisoners. The Tupamaros were destroyed from inside and outside by this violence. So that was the idea: how do you use violence in a revolutionary movement?

WRR: You've always favoured basing your screenplays on real stories.

C-G: Right. State of Siege I shot in Chile under Allende. I had several meetings with him, and he was a good man. He was trying to do something different in Latin America. And when I received the book about Horman (Missing is the story of American journalist Charles Horman, who disappeared in Chile in 1973) I said, "Ok, I will make a movie about people I met and appreciate." The American producers wanted me to make the whole story of Horman. I said no. The thing that interested me was when the father (Jack Lemmon) goes to look for his son, and he finds out that his son is different from what he thought and so is his country. He was a Republican who would vote for Nixon. So, what he finds out about his son's murder is all the more shocking. (American complicity in the Chilean coup and in Horman's death was later confirmed in documents declassified during the Clinton administration.)

WRR: What's the difference between working in Hollywood and Europe?

C-G: For me not much. I worked with the same European crew there. LA is a great place to work but not my favourite place to live. I've seen colleagues go there with high hopes and end up living a nightmare.

WRR: Charlie Chaplin comes to mind…Why is Z still relevant?

C-G: Why do you think so?

WRR: Because it's not about Greece in the 1960s. It's about us now.

In Search of Mike Tyson

Whenever you feel like criticizing anyone... just remember that all the people in this world haven't had the advantages that you've had.

F. Scott Fitzgerald, The Great Gatsby

1.

I'm searching for Mike Tyson. Late afternoon. I'm frantic. Jabbering to myself: 'Damn it you fool, where are those earmuffs?' I search my bag like airport security. No go. Hotel staff is watching me warily. After half a dozen Mike Tyson 'Black Energy' drinks (the promotion of which was the reason for his being in Poland) I was floating through the Westin Hotel lobby like a butterfly and buzzing like a bee. He'd been a prince at the press conference, handling questions like a diplomat on a foreign mission. Polite, not poisonous. His sunny disposition mirrored the suddenly dry and gorgeous spring weather he seemed to have imported from Las Vegas. No ear muffs. But what if? What if once we were alone in the conference room, just the two of us, the champ was in a mood to chomp?

No, no. That was the old Tyson who stayed a chameleon to me. I'd done my research. I'd seen him weep on Oprah and shake hands with Evander Holyfield, making a final public peace after all those years. I'd seen him talk about his new vegan diet with Ellen DeGeneres. The shy and retiring tyrannosaurus rex giving up meat! I had watched the James Toback film, Tyson, and all the biopics and other documentaries on offer. I had even suffered Will Smith singing I Think I Can Beat

Mike Tyson... And the fights, of course. Always the fights. That fight in 1987 when he decimated Trevor Berbick in less than two rounds to earn the championship was still imprinted on my brain. He was the youngest boxer to win the WBC, WBA and IBF heavyweight titles at 20 years, 4 months and 22 days old. Tyson won his first 19 professional bouts by knockout, with 12 of them occurring in the first round.

Awesome! Surely on his best day, Iron Mike could have beaten anyone who has ever graced the ring.

But where is he? We have an appointment for an exclusive interview at 5 pm, or was it after the press conference? The press conference is over. Holy Shit! I can't find him. Still searching...Now what was I going to ask him. My mind is blank. That bright sunshine is twisting my perception. It's hotter here today than in Miami or LA. Man oh man, it is hotter here than in Nicaragua.

The guy they first called Kid Dynamite and who later dubbed himself the "baddest" man on the planet is waiting somewhere in the hotel for me, and I can't find him.

The sickly kid with bad lungs rose up from the 'horrific' Brownsville, Brooklyn streets struggling, torn and frayed, bullied and scorned, training pigeons, his only friends (shades of Brando, the boxer, in On the Water Front), and turning to robbery to earn the respect of the older teens who taunted him because of his pudgy body, bespectacled aspect, his shy aversion to violence, his rootless confusion in the presence of a world without God, without motherly love, without fatherly concern.

Without. Enmeshed in hopeless conspiracy, he was captured thirty-eight times between the ages of ten and thirteen and given up to the law. At the age of 12 he was apprehended with 1500 bucks in his pocket. He of the famous ambidextrous, Thor-like punching and the soft-voiced, schoolboy lisp. He of the bipolar disposition. He of the very poor to very rich cliché. He who lost 300 million bucks. A raging bull now transformed into an aging street philosopher, unlettered yet well read. A conjurer of the ring, who now is doing his own Las Vegas revue which is headed for Broadway. A former party animal and juggler of women, who now follows the maxim of Benjamin Franklin: Early to bed, early to rise, makes a man healthy wealthy and wise. What to make of all these contradictions in one of the most outrageous and no doubt courageous figures of the late 20th Century. Why courageous? Because he was admittedly running scared the whole time. The eight-second knockout king with an inferiority complex…

Hells Bells! Mustn't keep the champ waiting. Maybe if I set off the fire alarm? That should put the cat among the pigeons!

All these thoughts are racing through my mind like greyhounds chasing a metallic rabbit.

2. Show me a hero, and I will write you a tragedy.

F. Scott Fitzgerald notebooks

He picked up boxing in reform school and when he got out, he went straight to Cus D'Amato, the legendary trainer of champions Floyd Patterson and Jose Torres. 'Do what I tell you to do and if it doesn't work then you can leave,' Cus said. Cus preached discipline and built up the kid's confidence. Fighting is spiritual, not physical. They kept each other alive. But Cus died 16 months before the kid won the championship in 1987. Sure, there was power, but there were also speed and accuracy and great bobbing and weaving defence.

(Let's rate the top ten boxers of all time: Joe Louis, Muhammad Ali, Sugar Ray Robinson, Jack Johnson, Tyson, Jack Dempsey, Julio Cesar Chavez, Rocky Marciano, Henry Armstrong Jr., and Willie Pep. Now your turn, dear reader.)

After Cus there was Don King, the bushy-headed intruder, who took over Tyson's career, ripped him off and sold him down the river. Things went over the cliff. The champ ran wild. He got married to Robin Givens. He stopped training. He got divorced. In 1990 he lost to Buster Douglas (42/1 underdog) in Tokyo. Maybe the greatest upset in boxing history. On the heels of that defeat there was his arrest for the rape of Desiree Washington. He was convicted and served three years of a six-year sentence. Some people say Don King set him up for the fall, supplying a tax attorney for defence counsel instead of a criminal lawyer. While in prison, Tyson wrote a letter to an ESPN boxing commentator saying basically that he would never admit to raping the woman, even if it lessened his time in prison, 'because I just didn't do it. However, there are about 5-7 other things I've done in my life which are far worse than that for which I am in prison for, so I feel I'm in the right place.'

It's hard to think of a better example of a victim of their own success than perhaps Tyson and his literary doppelganger, Fitzgerald. Success, marital problems and addiction spoiled both of them. A. [???]

History, like endurance, tells. Mike Tyson studies history. I know this from the press conference where he asked questions about Polish history. He wants to know. He seems endlessly curious, even surprised that he is still broke and still here. He reads—a habit he picked up in prison. He takes care of his wife and family. That is admittedly his main aim now. His third wife Lakiha Spicer is impressive. They got married ten days after his daughter, Exodus, died accidentally in 2009.

My phone rings finally. Mr. Tyson is waiting for me upstairs

Note to self: watch your ass.

3.

The victor belongs to the spoils.

F. Scott Fitzgerald, The Beautiful and the Damned

I push open the conference-room door, and there he is.

"Sorry I'm late," I say, "I couldn't find you." I'm actually early according to the five o'clock appointment time, but Mr. Tyson says: "Are you the one?"

"No, I mean yes, I'm here for the interview. But you are the one!"

Mike Tyson is seated at the table with his back to the window. He looks dapper in white cotton shirt and Brooks Brothers-style pale blue summer jacket. Following a vegan diet, he has trimmed 130 pounds from his still powerful frame. The shoulders and upper arms bulge from the jacket.

He still looks scary with the tribal tattoo. But he is smiling.

"Hey, this guy looks cool," he says to his personal assistant, David.

I swivel my head left and right with that 'Who Me?' look on my face. 'Take a seat, man and let's talk,' says Mr. Tyson.

I'm wearing sunglasses, a white shirt, a striped Boss summer blazer, shorts and black high-top converse sneakers without socks. So far so good.

'So where are you from, man? You aren't from here.'

'I'm from Atlanta amongst other places. Went to school there,' I say.'

'Atlanta's a great town,' he says.

Yeah, I liked it most of the time.' Atlanta is the hometown of Martin Luther King, of course, and Coca Cola and CNN and so forth. 'It's a real pleasure to meet you, especially since I interviewed Vladimir Klitschko last September,' I say.

'He was awesome, right?' says Tyson.

'He was a really great guy,' I say.

MT: He and his brother are amazing. I mean these guys are intellectuals and great boxers at the same time. That's why American people don't get them. You have to be a barbaric buffoon to be a champion in America. To be great you have to be a barbarian, not someone intellectual and stuff like that, because that is the quintessential boxing mode. When you get a guy like a Klitschko as a fighter, a smart fighter, it just doesn't fit the quintessential picture.'

WRR: It's very unusual.

MT: It's wonderful because when you think about it the baddest fighter in the world should be the smartest guy too. You know what I mean?

WRR: Well, Mike…Can I call you Mike?

MT: Sure.

WRR: Well, you have been pretty self-deprecating in the past. I've seen your interviews with Piers Morgan and Oprah where you shook hands with Holyfield. I've heard you say a lot of interesting things.

MT: You have to be self-deprecating in order to prevail…You know what I mean? You have to fight against all of the demons you're aware of. A lot of these guys are not aware of their demons. They are lost. A lot of these guys are not aware of someone else's feelings, and they think it's cool. They are accustomed to everyone paying them a lot of attention, but they don't pay attention. I don't mind so much if someone hurts people's feelings just because he's a prick. But let him be conscious of it. It's a disservice to both him and the other human being if he is hurting people without even paying attention to it. I rather him be conscious of it and be a prick than not be conscious and hurt someone out of ignorance or arrogance. It's all about knowing, you know what I mean, because once you know, then you know how you should be treated. It's like Cus was always telling me: People want to rule, but they don't want to serve. If you do become the champ or the king or someone important, how are you going to know how people should be treated if you can't serve. In order to rule you have to serve. Right?

WRR: Absolutely.

MT: How are you going to know how to treat other people unless you serve first? Some people never serve. They think—that word my wife always uses—they feel…what's the word…entitlement. Once you know life, you know that you are just another grain of sand in the world. People don't like the fact that they don't have control of a situation. I don't care how much money they've got; they don't have control over someone they love dying. You know what I mean?

WRR: Yes, we don't have control over the ultimate thing.

Immediately a picture pops into my head of a dear friend of mine who has contracted cancer at the age of 35. Distance. Things come and go.

MT: There's no way you can control uncertainty, and we still yearn to grasp at…It's never been done. The pharaohs didn't do it. No one did it. But we think we can do it. That's our vanity.

WRR: What's it like to be in your position? Both famous and infamous at the same time?

(I'm surprised to hear my own voice sounding like Johnny Depp doing Hunter S. Thompson. Am

I under the influence of all that Black Energy? Holy Jesus! Maintain, man! Maintain!)

MT: I approach it from a philosophical point of view. Because when you are at that level you are sure you can't die so, you are surprised when something comes back at you.

WRR: You were incredibly young when the world started coming at you or maybe the other way round. Champion at 20. Extraordinary. It's easy to be troubled at that age. I was.

MT: Sure, because I bought everything that Cus told me. I thought I was Dionysus. I thought I was Alexander the Great. I really looked at life from that perspective.

WRR: But weren't you in a sense?

MT: No. But I looked at life from that perspective. I don't look at myself the way others do. 'Oh wow, Mike is the greatest! Oh my god, we love mike.' No, I look at myself for what I am. I had a bad upbringing, and I can be real dark at times, but I don't want to. I want to live on the light side of life, of passion and love, you know what I mean? Because I know I'm dark and that at my core. I'm dark and bad.

WRR: But is that true really? Do you really believe that about yourself, this Manichean, this good and evil part? The ring is different, but you don't seem that way to me. It is true?

MT: Yes. Boxing is like a cock fight. It is brutal and bloody. There is shame in it, and yet there are rules to abide by. Now Tyson seems tame yet still dangerous like the tiger he kept. He keeps his rage within him like a pet. Don't we all do that to differing degrees? A curious species these human beings are.

WRR: Was it your upbringing?

MT: Yeah. It was tough. It was Cus, too. Something must have happened to Cus because Cus believed in not taking any shit from anybody. You had to be careful what you said around him. He sponsored me all that time, and he was such a disciplinarian and a cold, cruel guy. Tough, but he's sensitive. Like me. Sometimes I want to cry, but you can never tell by the way I am towards someone else. You know that's my situation. I had to learn to be cold and cruel, and yet I'm sensitive and I can cry. People don't expect that.

WRR: I saw you on Oprah. (Thank God for YouTube.) That was a tough one.

MT: Well, I'm just that kind of guy. When I was with Cus he would tell me that feelings were nothing. Feelings are just feelings like being hungry or thirsty. He used to say what do you do when you are hungry or thirsty? Do you wait for food to come? Or do you eat? Just do it. Cus said that before Nike. Forget the feelings. Just do it.

4. Either you think — or else others have to think for you and take power from you, pervert and discipline your natural tastes, civilize and sterilize you.

F. Scott Fitzgerald, Tender Is the Night

WRR: Just to switch tracks since we have limited time, I wanted to ask you about your Las Vegas show. Is that all right?

MT: Yes, it's six days. A sold-out show. Spike Lee called me the other day and said that he has a producer who wants to bring it to Broadway, and he's never even seen my show. All he saw was reviews.

WRR: So, what do you do in the show?

MT: This is me talking about a dynamic collection of stories that you know about, but you don't know the inside story. I talk about my divorce, and you know about the divorce. But you don't know that every day we were sleeping with each other, and then going to court and saying, 'She's a bitch and he's beating me up.'

WRR: What was that all about?

MT: Just stupid kids with too much money. It doesn't have anything to do with real emotions. You know what I mean? So, I'm talking about that, and my rape case conviction and about my mother and my father. This is so interesting. I don't know who my mother and father are. I mean their real names. What are they communists? Reds? They never told me their real names. My mother's name is not Lorna Tyson. I don't even know her name. They lied. I don't know who my parents are and their real names even. The guy named Tyson on my birth certificate is not my father. He claims to be my father, but he's not. I don't even know who I am. I don't even know how old I am. One of my birth certificates says '66 and another says '67. How do I go to my family tree? How do I discover where I came from? I mean who the hell is Tyson? I'm not a Tyson. Who the hell is Tyson?

WRR: Does it really matter to you now?

MT: No, it doesn't, and it does. Personally, it does. I'm a made-up entity.

WRR: What is humorous in the show?

MT: Talking about Robin and us having sex all the time. Like after the divorce, I went to her house one day, and she pulls up with Brad Pitt and shit…Oh, man my dick was so hard, and then it went limp like a wet noodle when I saw them together.

WRR: Do you know Brad Pitt?

MT: I don't think I met him, no.

WRR: You've been doing some acting. Ever thought about Shakespeare? That could be fun.

MT: Othello? (laughs)

WRR: That might be typecasting.

MT: Hmmm I don't know. I think I could play the fat, venomous toad.

At this point there is a lot of laughter and I'm glad he didn't take offense at my question. I mean really. Tyson in Shakespeare. What is wrong with me?

MT: I'm not kidding. Shakespeare talks about the fat venomous toad, and maybe he had someone like me in mind.

The photographer is snapping away. I'm bobbing and weaving. We pause now to take a photo of Mike and me doing a toast with tins of Black Energy. I'm thinking speed and accuracy are just as important to the writer under pressure as they are to the boxer. This is a match after all. We are feeling each other out. But if the champ is benevolent, then so am I. Words can be as swift and deadly as fists or hmmm… teeth.

21

MT: They have all these energy drinks here. I think they need one called Soul Pole. More laughter.

WRR: I like Soul Pole. That's good. I won't write it so that you can trademark it. Actually, I should write it because then everyone will know it's your idea and be too afraid to steal it lest the Toad descend on them with his venom, what?

MT: Sooooul Poooooole.

WRR: How did this project come about?

MT: I have no idea. I found out it was Black Energy when I saw the car downstairs. But I thought, 'This is awesome!'

I'm really starting to like this guy.

WRR: It was so top secret that I didn't even know what the subject of your visit was until two days ago

MT: Me either. I had no idea. Last time I was in Spain shooting for Fiat (a TV advert for Panda). Before, I was a pariah, and nobody wanted to look at me. And now all these people want to use me. That goes back to being poor, and maybe now being rich again. What the hell? They like me now?

WRR: You proved F Scott Fitzgerald wrong. I'm sure you've heard the cliché, 'There are no second acts in American lives.' I never believed that. I don't think Fitzgerald did either. I think that life and especially American life is all about an endless series of second chances.

MT: He was a very depressed, manic type of guy. His wife was insane, you know what I mean? They were some party animals, though. He didn't embrace his homosexuality, Scott Fitzgerald, you know what I mean? Zelda made him comfortable. It's a shame, she went insane. I think about him a lot. You know the house he used in The Great Gatsby. That was Otto Kahn's house. That huge house. He was a big banker, but he moved out to Long Island because his neighbours in New Jersey didn't like him because he was Jewish. That was sick, but that's the way it was back then. I always look at that house and think about the book.

The Jazz Age writer, F. Scott Fitzgerald, whom Tyson admires, was the icon of 1920s New York, much as Tyson was in the late 1980s. Fitzgerald, like Tyson, was washed up and broke by the age of 40. All of his books out of print. If Fitzgerald epitomized the Jazz Age elite in New York, perhaps the same could be said of Tyson about the sinister beat of the Rap Age. Tenuous maybe, but food for thought. Tyson was certainly an outrageous, self-promoting icon as was Fitzgerald. And how fitting is it that he made his comeback playing himself in a movie called The

Hangover. Comparisons can be odious but still...Like Fitzgerald, Tyson sacrificed his talent to celebrity, money and addiction.

WRR: Have you been to this part of the world before?

MT: Never been to Poland. But I've been to Moscow, Spain, Istanbul, Slovakia, Finland. I was in Chechnya.

WRR: That was dangerous.

MT: That's the kind of guy I am. If I'm not doing something where I can get obliterated, then I won't do it.

WRR: Have you changed then? Do you now have better control of the animal that lives inside all of us? Have you thought of some deeper purpose?

MT: You know what I wanted to do with my life, but then I have the kids... What I wanted was to be a missionary. I was thinking about that recently. About five years ago.

WRR: Why?

MT: I felt my life was a waste. If I wasn't doing anything for myself, I thought that at least I should help people. You know, go to Chechnya or some of these places. I dated a missionary. They have their own little thing going. It's just what they do...They help people... I don't know. We all provide from different perspectives.

WRR: How important is Islam to you? You converted as did Muhammad Ali. Is he a hero?

MT: He is everyone's hero...When I think about Islam, I think from this perspective: I believe Allah is God. I believe Allah created you. Allah created the planet. Allah created everything. I believe it's wrong to kill any of God's creations. That's what I believe. Do you think I think Allah wants what's going on in Israel now? All that is ridiculous. That is all about power. People kill over religion.

WRR: You are taking the Christopher Hitchens line now that religion poisons things.

MT: All I know from history is that a lot of people died over God. But God is here for life. God's not here for death.

WRR: Maybe you need to do what George Foreman's done. (Become a preacher.)

MT: No, that's not who I am. I'm just the kind of guy who is going to tell you black is black and white is white...And people won't like me because of that. I'm not politically correct. That's what fucked my life up. Not being politically correct.

WRR: (softly like a radio playing in the background) Well there were probably a few drugs in there and a lot of money …

MT: I'm never gonna be that kind of guy…I'm just not that kind of guy. I'm never going to say what the masses believe if I don't think it's true. I'm not going to do that.

WRR: Speaking of losing lots of money, which we weren't…You know I have a friend who lost $70 million in less than ten years.

Tyson laughs.

MT: I lost much more than that.

He is really tickled now.

MT: Nigger ahaaaaa ha ha ha ha…

WRR: I told him I'm going to interview Mike Tyson pretty soon, and I said to him you're obviously not as smart as Tyson is, because you couldn't make as much to lose.

MT: Tell him I lose that in a year…

WRR: But you are getting it back. Getting some of it back anyway.

MT: Man, it's not about money. It's not money. It's the greed that gets people.

WRR: Alright then. You fought figuratively and literally for what you've got. How do you deal with greed and with power?

MT: You despise it. The strong should do what the weak do. The weak despise what they can't consume. They can't consume power or wealth. They hate or despise it. They find a reason to believe that it's bad and it's crippling the world. It might or might not be true. But they find a reason. They fight the battle by despising it. There is a pause while this sinks in. Time is running.

WRR: Is boxing show business?

MT: Yes

WRR: Are you like a stunt man?

MT: No. I'm not a stunt man. I'm a magician. I'm an illusionist. I make you believe something is happening that is not actually happening.

WRR: How do you do that?

MT: It starts before the press conference. I tell you everything that I'm going to do to you. I saw myself as king of the fight world because I had had a miserable life and to me it was like the miserable shall inherit the crown. My opponent is a dog at my feet. That's how I would do it.

WRR: So, you would transform yourself. Like Ali.

MT: Ali wasn't good at intimidation, but he was good at making people believe what he said was true.

WRR: Did you learn some of that from him?

MT: Pretty much. But when people ask me which fighter, I'm closest to, I say Roberto Duran. I took Ali for what he was. Roberto Duran represents me. Ali is tall and beautiful and elegant as a fighter. I'm short and ugly. Ali was very dignified. He doesn't curse. I tell people to suck my dick, you bitch. Motherfucker. That's my language. Roberto Duran talks like that. He grew up tough. Ali is the greatest fighter who ever lived, and he never had a street fight. Never. That was his confidence. Confidence breeds success and success breeds confidence.

WRR: Hand in hand.

MT: Confidence applied properly becomes genius. There is nothing like confidence. For instance, take a woman or a man, anyone you want, and give them all the qualities of success: big dick, big brain, beautiful body, whatever it is that when you see them makes you think they are going to make it… Give them all of it. Finance. Wealth. All of it. But don't give them confidence. Now push them out into the world. And they fail. Now, you strip away all of those assets. Then push him or her out into the world, and they succeed. That's how it goes. I don't know why. But that's how it goes.

WRR: It's not the closed door that you concentrate on. It's rather opening the door. You said that in an earlier interview somewhere.

MT: Yes. People are so busy looking at the closed door that they don't see how to open the one right in front of them. 'Why did they close the door on me? I deserve more! I'm entitled. I'm more educated!' Forget it. Just look for how to open the door. Of course, you don't give up, if it doesn't open the first time. Take an actor who goes for auditions. They have been working for ten years. If they don't get the role, does that mean that all they did is done in vain? No! Keep doing the work. Keep doing it until that door opens. It will open if you keep knocking…and if it doesn't then break it open.

WRR: Deafness to the word No.

MT: Yes. The power of the word No is so strong, it's hard to be deaf to it. You understand No before you understand Yes. No has such an overwhelming effect on you. (Laughs) It's overwhelming. It's crazy how much power that word has: NOOOO! So don't listen to the people who tell you No.

And with that David says it's time to go. They have more meetings.

WRR: Thank you, sir, for your time.

MT: Thank you, brother.

Mike Tyson has only been in town for a few hours. There are promotions to do. There is money to be made on the comeback trail, even in a place as strange as Poland.

* * *

Note: At his request, Mr. Tyson is now reading God's Playground, the excellent history of Poland penned by Norman Davies and presented to him by your correspondent. (I gave him a copy of my book, too, just in case you were wondering. Peace.)

Fun Lovin' Criminal Behavior

Sunday. 6 a.m., the first of May. It was cold and the wind was blowing 20 knots. Ah yes, early Spring in Poland. I'm standing outside Spatif in Sopot chatting with the inimitable Huey Morgan, a fun lovin' criminal if ever I saw one.

Huey is cool. There! I said it. But then that's what everyone says. And you know what? They are right. Shit! Even Barry White thought Huey was cool. He wrote in his autobiography that he used to play the Fun Lovin Criminals's Love Unlimited before he went on stage just to tweak his mood.

Now Huey—that's what everyone calls him—was talking in his rocky Brooklyn accent about his encounter with the man from Atlanta who invented funk. (I thought that was George Clinton) "So we had just come off the stage at this festival and James Brown walks up to and says, I don't know what it was, but it was fun! Then he just turned and walked away."

"That was it?" I said.

"Yeah, and our manager at the time hurries over and goes, what happened with James? What did he say? He thought James was pissed off. I said: he told me we were funky."

"Hey, man you have to tell me something about your music," he says. "You remember that scene at the end of Casablanca?"

"Yeah. Bogart and the French police guy, Louis."

"Huey, I think this could be the beginning of a beautiful friendship. By the way, what happened to Fast and Frank?" I say.

"They stayed at the hotel. They asked me to bring some girls back. Would I do that for them?" "Nah." We both say it at the same time.

* * *

Love Unlimited

Barry White, saved my life/And if Barry White, saved your life/ Or got you back with your ex-wife/Sing Barry White, Barry White, it's alright... Friday. It started innocently enough. We sped to the coast up Route 7 from the capital in a Smart car. JB was my driver. We checked into the Radisson in Gdansk at 11p.m. Then we went to Karl's place, Absinthe, in the Old Town. My bodyguard, PG, who had been commentating on the Royal Wedding in Warsaw early in the day, arrived at midnight.

Absinthe was jumping as usual. The Deejay, a local singer called Anna, was spinning love. Then we got a call from FLC's manager to come hang out in Sopot. Too late. The wine was already in the glass.

Late that night after many more glasses—my driver, JB, is a big drinker—there was a minor scuffle ending with some huge bald guy getting me in a choke hold from behind. Rock and roll.

PG, who holds a black belt in Tao, pulled the guy off of me.

The guy must have decided we were ok. Right away he pressed a beer into our hands and made up by kissing me Soviet style on the mouth. Not bad. Affection demands respect.

We rolled into the hotel at 5a.m. We were ready to meet the Criminals.

* * *

We Have All the Time in the World

We have all the time in the world/Time enough for life/To unfold/ All the precious things Saturday. Everything is set. 5p.m. sound check. 6p.m. meet the band and talk. 10p.m. concert.

We walk in. FLC is onstage checking sound. Huey Morgan working over his guitar. Fast doing his thing. Frank banging the drum slowly and loudly.

"Huey's wearing Aviators, too," said PG as he offered me a fine tobacco product.

"Obviously a man of taste," I said. A good omen.

Huey Morgan (guitar/vocal), Brian Leiser (bass/keyboards/harmonica, trumpet) and their present drummer, Frank Benbini, are the

British-based musicians who invented their special brand of alternative fusion employing rock, blues and funk and hip-hop lyric line that is still—especially live— as irresistible as it is unique. Huey and Brian a.k.a. "Fast" are New Yorkers who live in London. Frank's a Brit from the Midlands.

While FLC went through the motions, we retreated upstairs to drink some of the band's tequila in order to better interrogate the Criminals. Soon they joined us around a big table full of various snacks, none of them Scoobies. Everyone helped themselves to drinks.

The Criminals have a history in Poland. They have played here a couple of dozen times and Huey makes forays as a deejay from time to time. They played one of their first Polish gigs at a prison in Krakow in '96.

How did that gig happen?

Huey: "I always thought it was cool how Johnny Cash played (San) Quentin and basically, we wanted to do a promo for our record and asked are there any prisons we could play in. So, they said, we can get you one in Poland…(all laugh). We thought it would be cool because a lot of people are in jail not for violence but for drug offences. We just went and played in the prison yard… Everyone was cool but there was this one guy at the front who gave us the finger, so I shouted at him, when you get back in there, everyone is going to sodomize you, and the place went crazy. Yeah, everyone else was cool. All the high security guys were up in their cells, but it was cool because a lot of the guys were like English dudes who had got caught smuggling or whatever, so they knew the music and also people in jail have radios…It was kind of strange having criminals cheering for criminal songs. We were playing 'Scooby Snacks' and they were singing along."

Fast: "The Polish audience is cool. We've played here so many times I've lost track." Scooby Snacks, from their first album, Come Find Yourself (1996), is the seminal FLC song with its anthem chorus about robbing banks while high on Valium. (Their biggest hit to date is Loco, which reached #5 on the British charts in 2001.) The record flopped in the US but went to number seven in the UK and FLC, like Bill Hicks, the great American comedian, became instant stars in Britain and Ireland, while being ignored back home.

They released the latest of their six albums, Classic Fantastic, in 2010 on their own label funded by private investors. The release followed a five-year legal battle with their former manager. The album is a blast from the past with a contemporary spin implementing multiple instruments including brass and strings with a modernized 70s groove, all packaged with the patented FLC bravado, which still says: "Stick 'em up punk. We're the Fun Lovin' Criminals." We the Three, from the same record, might be termed the band's update of their eponymous Fun Lovin' Criminals song from the first album.

Surprising perhaps for other bands, this is a perfect summer party record without a hint of angst following their half-decade in the recording wilderness.

Huey is sitting on my left. PG sits opposite looking like a white-man version of a bling-bling bouncer. Daddy got style. Fast and Frank are sitting way down at the end of the table and the tour manager, Pete Dempsey, wanders up and down while we talk.

"What are you doing between now and the concert?" I ask.

"I like to chill before gigs and meditate," says Frank.

"Frank's into heavy meditation," says Huey. "So, we'll go back to the hotel and chill and put our suits on."

"Well, that famous guru died this week, didn't he?" I said "Baba Raba Ding Dong.

The one with the crazy hair. Guru to the stars. Produced jewellery from his mouth. Do you know who I mean?"

Frank says: "Oh yeah, yeah. I heard that. But I'm not a nutcase about it all."

"How do you like London?"

"London's a cool place to live," says Huey. "How did you get from London to here?"

"How did you get started playing guitar?"

"Good question," says Huey. "People don't ask me that much... It started out in school. I was in seventh grade and there were some kids older than us who had instruments. Some guy started playing Jumpin' Jack Flash and every little hair on my body stood up and I said I've got to be able to do that...It was the first time I actually wanted to do something other than what I had to do. You have to go to school. You have to do your chores. That was a key moment. Also, I listened to my mother's records. She had really good taste. She had some really good records at home. She had Ray Charles and BB King. All of that stuff."

"Didn't B. B. King play on one of your records?"

Huey: "He played with us on Mini Bar blues when we were recording 100% Columbian. He was really cool. I play a guitar called a Chet Atkins, a Gibson Chet Atkins, and BB King waved me over in the studio and said "Lemme see that guitar boy." And so, I went over, and he just hands me Lucille. That's like the crown jewels. He looked at the way I was holding it and said, "Son, hold it like a woman." It was like "What's the matter with you boy, hold that things like a woman." So, I was holding Lucille like a woman, and he was strumming my guitar. And he said he'd like to play with us. So, we said sure we'll send you a track, and if you like it lay something down for us. So, he gave us a couple of solos."

"How did you and Fast get together? You were working at Limelight, right?"

"He was answering phones and I was clearing tables. You know, when we got together Fast was into a lot of electronic music like Depeche Mode and stuff I didn't really know. And I think that's how we got our sound. He was making basic electronic music that gave us our beat. He was messing around at the apartment because we lived together, worked together. For example, he turned me on to electronic music and I turned him onto Tom Petty. Then he turned me onto J. J. Cale later and I turned him onto some hip hop. It's cool because we all like different types of music. We listened to a lot of the classics. Our style always confused music journalists."

I say: "You are preaching to the choir with me."

Fast says: "People who like our music like ten different styles all at once. Hip hop, rock, blues, love songs. We blend it together. That's what we do."

WRR: "That's cool. By the way, are you going to play the Louis Armstrong tonight?"

Huey: "Are we playing All the time in the World? It always goes kind of how the crowd likes. We play not to the crowd but for the crowd. We try to feel the crowd out and see what they want and give them what they need. If we play a mellow song and see they aren't into it, then we say, ok. They aren't into that shit. They want to rock out. So, then we play the heavier stuff. We must play the Louis Armstrong song because that is one of our favourite songs."

Frankie: "I just put it into the list!"

WRR: "Thanks, I really would enjoy that."

Fast is looking over the set list.

Huey: Let me see that. I'm old, man. I need to see that shit. There is a tape going round in my brain and I have to access those files…. Hey (looking over the list) this is a rocking show. This is a pretty ass-kicking show, man. We the Three is a new track from Plastic Fantastic. Here's

All the Time in the World. I guess you like that because it sounds kind of like a David Lynch soundtrack… Fast and his trumpet. You'll hear it tonight… I didn't even know that Fast played trumpet until we already had a record deal. We were sitting around as we are now, and he says I can play trumpet.

Fast: I enjoy the trumpet.

Huey: He has a signature sound. Every time we add the trumpet in the studio, Fast says it sounds like Ben Hur.

Fast: Ba ba ba ba! Ba da da da da da!

WRR: I hear Romans in that.

I Can't Get with That.

They try to move us/to use us/like Judas did to Jesus

Hugh Thomas Angel Diaz Morgan is a serious guy. Half Puerto Rican, half Irish, his father died in Vietnam in 1972. He followed his father into the military at 18 when the law like a tough godfather made him "an offer he couldn't refuse." Go to jail or join up. He chose the Marines where he became an underwater demolition frogman. Translate SEAL, the same guys who got Bin Laden. He's an award-winning radio deejay: his show, called Huey After Midnight, runs on BB2 on Fridays.

Huey: It's easier for me to talk to a musician because I am a musician so that might be responsible for my success. I play music that's fun to play. I can play anything: hip hop, jazz, some obscure blues thing that nobody ever heard before. I can play classics and old disco shit and people like it. They like the eclecticism of it all. It's like what we were talking about downstairs. To be in this band is great too, because we get to play all kinds of music. We are playing jazz, hip-hop, rock, thrash. For a musician that's fun. That nice big old Marshall amp helps too."

Huey also is an occasional TV performer and movie actor. He was in 2007's Headrush, which Variety called "brash breezy and irreverently funny including Fun Lovin' Criminals singer Huey Morgan as a Tarantino-type mobster."

"I played a transvestite," says Huey. "So, I had to learn to walk and run in high heels. If the director had told me more about the part before I flew in, I might have punched him." He laughs.

WRR: What about the state of the music industry these days?

Huey: "The record companies are still called record companies, but no one buys records. These days fans come and go at the blink of an eye, so we've learned to please ourselves. That's why we self-released our last album. We are aware that music can be downloaded for free, so it's not a matter of selling records anymore. It's about making new music and trying it out on people. If they like it, then they can catch us live… because that's what we like best."

WRR: "Um…I have to ask you. Do you have any Scooby snacks in your possession?"

Huey: "No I do not."

Fast: "That has a lot of different meanings."

WRR: "This is funny. I was thinking what is this Scooby snack thing? I knew it wasn't what Scooby Doo chows down on, so I looked it up."

Huey: "What did you come up with?"

Me: "It said Valium. But I prefer Xanax, by prescription only of course, if I'm going down that road."

Fast: "I prefer animal tranquilizers."

Huey: "He takes dog medicine."

Fast: "Nah, nah."

WRR: "No. Do you really use that?"

Huey: "He does."

Fast: "I took one on a long trip once."

Huey: "On long trips Scoobies are good. I took a couple on a long flight and woke up in Sydney."

WRR: By the way, I happen to have some Xanax as a present for you guys. You won't have to deprive a dog tonight, Fast!"

Huey: "I'll take one of those, for when I go to sleep. That is nice of you man. Very cool bro."

Fast: "Scooby snacks have been exchanged."

Everyone laughs.

WRR: "You have a great solo on I Can't Get with That…"

Huey: Thanks, man. That was the first time I actually wrote a solo. Usually, we do an improv thing and keep a solo if it's good. But with that one I actually set out to do it that way as a key part of the song. When we play that song, I always play the solo that way."

WRR: What about Big Night Out?

Huey: That was a Tom Petty and the Heartbreakers thing. I actually wrote a handwritten letter to Tom Petty to get permission to use stuff in that song. Tom wrote us a letter back and said he ripped that riff off a disco song!

WRR: "Who's making the best music now? Britain or America?

Huey: "I think the place is America because it's so wide open. In England it's all chart stuff and there's so much turnover with bands because the record companies are getting desperate… they take a chunk of everything, the touring, the merchandising. They sign a whole bunch of bands and if the single doesn't hit the charts, "Next". There's always another band."

WRR: That's the problem with all these music contest shows. You get people who have no management. It's free entertainment. It's disposable. You pick a winner. The other thing is that everything sounds the same.

Huey: Yeah, if you're watching something like Pop Idol or American Idol, the guy who is the least eccentric and more white-bread and homogenized is the guy or girl who is going to win because that's who they think they can sell to a wider fan base.

* * *

Big Night Out

Axamillion morals, difference in opinion/I was with him/he had 7 Jack and cokes in him…Tequila was my poison, but I think Huey was on Jack and Coke. The concert was great. Huey said: "I thought it was off the hook." There was even a mosh pit for a couple of songs. FLC has a super model on their "D, " for sure. They are still one of the best live acts around. The after party moved from Fabrika to Absinthe and then about 3a.m. Huey and Pete said, "Come with us to Sopot." I did. The rest is history.

Rutger Hauer: Surfing the Blue Screen

It's 5 p.m. Monday and we are waiting for Rutger Hauer on the third floor of the Hotel InterContinental in Warsaw. He's not late. We're early. He's just flown in from Amsterdam for the press conference before the Polish premier of Lech Majewski's The Mill and the Cross, the brilliantly imaginative cinematic portrait of Dutch master Peter Bruegel's The Way to Calvary (1564). Hauer plays Bruegel in the film, which also stars Charlotte Rampling and Michael

York. Variety, the Hollywood movie magazine, called the film "an extraordinary imaginative leap... (combining) old and new technologies allowing the viewer to live inside the painting." Majewski's film did well at Sundance, where Robert Redford, who started his career as an artist, praised the film.

Now Rutger Hauer (RH), veteran of 60-some films over 40 years, including a selection of seminal screen villains (Roy Batty, the Hitcher, Cardinal Rourke) is basking in something of a renaissance. His other film at Sundance is a nasty little Grindhouse production made in Canada called Hobo with a Shotgun, a noir thriller based loosely on Dashiell Hammett's classic novel, Red Harvest. Anyway, while I'm waiting. I'm in jeans, black leather jacket, black leather converse high tops and of course, Oakley chromatic sunglasses.

Then this young girl reporter comes up to me and introduces herself.

She says: "I wonder if I could ask you about how you prepared for your role in this film?" She thinks I'm him.

Without missing a beat, I start in, "That's a good question. Every role is different, and I am different in every role, even though it's always me, of course. I draw on my inner resources and some method exercises. For instance, for this film, I copied several of Bruegel's paintings—a half dozen or so. I also ate nothing but porridge and rotten vegetables for a month, just to capture the early 16th century feel." Etcetera. Etc.

On cue R H tacked to my left, sailing by into the press conference. He was wearing the exact same shoes as I was—those Converse. He wears a black suit with a black scarf with polka dots and above all a warm smile.

The girl reporter's eyes go back and forth from him to me. Her mouth drops open. "I thought because of the sunglasses…" she said.

"No problem," I said. "Rutger's used to it."

Another hackette bites the dust.

The real Rutger Hauer grew up in Amsterdam. He ran away to sea at 15 to work on a freighter. He later worked as an electrician and carpenter, while studying drama at night.

He then joined an experimental acting troupe for five years before making his name as the lead in the 1969 hit Dutch TV show Floris, directed by Paul Verhoeven. "I was a wild man back then," says RH. The pair would go on to make a series of films together including R.H.'s favourite film, Turkish Delight (1973), voted best Dutch film ever.

"It was not only a wonderful film, but it was also my first film and that gives it a special place in my heart," he says R.H. became known in the U.S. after playing a German terrorist opposite Sylvester Stallone in Nighthawks in 1981. He was soon asked to star in Das Boot, the German submarine epic. But he turned it down. "I didn't want to be typecast as a German heavy. I never thought I'd have a career after Nighthawks. I had a bad time," he says.

Das Boot went on to be a smash hit worldwide, making Jurgen Prochnau a star.

Never mind. That same year RH made Blade Runner, perhaps the greatest sci-fi movie of them all, based on a Philip K. Dick novel and directed by Ridley Scott.

Here's the thing. I might as well confess I had no idea whether RH would even talk to me one on one. It wasn't scheduled, which is almost always fun. It gets you that nice little adrenalin boost. Majewski pulled some strings. He pulled RH away from a face-full of microphones.

* * *

"Come in. Come in," he says.

It's Tuesday morning at 10 a.m. Pretty soon I'm drinking coffee and smoking Camels with RH in his suite at the InterContinental. Interviewing celebs can be a nasty business. But RH is cool baby, cool. I don't have much time, so we start immediately, now excellent replicants, programmed to meet deadlines.

What was it like working with Lech Majewski on the Bruegel film?

"The decision to work with someone happens in the first 30 seconds. I seem to always know instinctively... And this project was so different, so revolutionary... You become paint in such a film. Paintings were there before photos of course. Anyway, film is sort of our version of painting now: I see a link in Lech diving into a painting, into an ancient form with a digital format. That's the trick. Do you know that 95% of the films at Sundance are digital? That's where it is. And it's not going to go away. We're in a big transition... On the set—what set in fact? We were swimming in a blue screen. Lech showed us where we would be in the picture and then we had to trust the blue screen..."

Is this film a revolution?

"Yes!"

Did you enjoy working in Poland?

"Yes, I did, and I will be back again much sooner than you think. If you don't mind, I'd like to tell you about this project. This is the moment to talk about this fucking dream. If it doesn't become a little more real than it will become my hobby. I have something called the Rutger Hauer Film Factory. It's basically a sweatshop for filmmakers that you can really do anywhere. I've done it three years in Holland, but they aren't spending any money. They're tight." (laughs)

How does it work?

"The young filmmakers follow my guidelines to learn to make films faster and more economically and that's all it is. It's nothing to do with art. Art comes in when the filmmaker is an artist. This is about mechanics and the filmmaking process... I want to show them how not to get turned sideways too much because of commercial values. They're okay. But in this business, nobody knows what really works. I've heard it for 35 years, and I still don't understand what the fuck they are talking about. You just have to want to make good films... So, if people want to know more about this project—which I hope will also take place in Poland—it's all there on the internet. You know I've had this real warm feeling for Poland for a while and Poland may just be ready to embrace this idea and that's why I'll be coming back."

What's the driving force in this project?

"It's a professional lobby, if you like, a chance to say to my younger peers, "Come join me and have a good time. I want filmmakers to learn how to work on instinct and not on brain power or ego or dick power because if you leave all that behind you will be amazed what you can do. This creative animal is inside you, inside everybody to some extent. If you go, there you will be surprised and that's it. I send them home from the workshop with at least two short films. If your readers want to know about this, then they need to go to filmfactoryshorts.com. Google that and you will find my channel. You can also simply Google Rutger Hauer. We're running out of time here. Why don't you meet me here at 3:30 and you can go with me to the airport? Then we can talk some more."

For a moment I think about The Hitcher, the movie in which he plays the murderous hitchhiker from hell and wonder if riding in a car with RH is such a good idea. He put the scare in scary after all.

"With pleasure," I say. Show business calls for sacrifices.

We move over to the desk while RH shows me the website. The waiter arrives to bring more coffee and RH orders some Camels, regular not light.

* * *

On the way to the airport... So what movies are you doing these days. Isn't this something of a renaissance for you?

"That's true. I'm starting to shoot the movie tomorrow in Holland about the kidnapping of the Heineken heir back in the 1980s. It's my first Dutch film in years."

But aren't you the Dutch Eastwood, Bogart and McQueen rolled into one?

"Absolutely!"

How was Sundance?

"I had never been in the festival. I'd been in the 'lab.' But this time I was there for the worldwide openings for Mill and Hobo. They are both art films. Hobo is a ready-to-wear cult movie. You will see some relation to the 'Hitcher' and the 'Blade Runner' characters. I ran onto the stage at the Sundance screening with a shotgun during the opening credits and shouted, "Hey, this thing ain't loaded!" Shotgun already had distribution and we didn't know if Lech's film would. You roll the dice...But now it's crawling into the world. It's an experimental film that needs to be seen. You know what the hard part about the visual medium is? Do you want to talk about a poem? Well, some films are poems. Lech's film is a painted poem. Let's leave it at that… It's so hard to talk about 'cause you don't want to kill the essence…I really feel you need to keep it open and not dictate what people should see."

One of the great Hollywood stories is about how you changed the monologue at the end of Blade Runner. Is that true?

"I did work on it to make a simpler version. That's very much part of my talent. I tend to like what is not written, what is usually not filmed. In Roy's last words there was a page of like 300 words or something. It was a really looooong speech. But I thought after four big opera-style deaths we needed to go very quickly, or the audience would see the end coming. And that ruins everything… So, I cut all the lines except two— it was after midnight when we were shooting. I thought what if I could wrap up the character in one sentence. I chopped it down to: "I've seen things you people wouldn't believe. Attack ships on fire off the shoulder of Orion. I've watched c-beams glitter in the dark near the Tannhäuser Gate. All those … moments will be lost in time, like tears…in rain. "

I cut 40 or 50 lines—but what I really wrote was the silence of the scene. For me to sit there at fourin the morning on one of the last days on the shoot, well this was me and Roy fighting for a moment. and for the line to travel for all those years into people like a fucking arrow. I'm so happy that it meant something. It was fun you know. I danced through that movie… This movie really liberated me because as an actor I felt I was really in the right place with the right director, and I worked hard to do some crazy, funny, excellent work."

What's on the agenda now?

"Well, it's a crazy busy time and I love it. I have six movies coming out in the first four months of this year. They are all completely different and really interesting and some of them are really beautiful. I'm including Hobo. It's dirty and ugly and over the top. The scenes are all like a mini soap opera. Hobo is a blast where everything we do is wrong. It's a kind of western, but everything is fucked up. So, there's this guy who walks with a cane who is very simple but has this basic idea of justice and pretty soon that cane is going to be a shotgun."

I already like it. Is surfing the blue screen as you did in The Mill and the Cross the wave of the future?

"It has to be. You know Sin City is using the same elements. It's about a cartoon, like The Mill is about a painting. Sin City is all green screen and it's done in one room. It's a great idea to make a movie in one room. Hey! Don't step in this room cause were making a movie here! Beautiful…The trick is you have one green or blue screen and one camera and then we put things in there and organize it later. It's like you sing your songs in a headset. You don't need to have all the musicians there, do you?"

Definitely. We are living in a virtual reality.

"Sure, sure. What the fuck else are we? Come on though. We aren't even virtual really. We are just pixels.

Jon Lord: Smoke on the Keyboard

"Let's see what kind of trouble we can get into," says Jon Lord as we prepare to sit down in the conference room of the InterContinental in beautiful downtown Warsaw at midday, the day of his concert in the Hala Kongresowa.

That's music to my ears from the keyboard player of the seminal rock group Deep Purple, or Purple as he calls them. The last few days, ever since I'd heard I'd got this gig, I've had the opening riff from My Woman from Tokyo thumping through my mind's ear. And here's the guy who wrote it? He played Hammond for the loudest rock band in the world, a band that to date has sold over 100,000,000 recordings. Give me a musician any time or a film director to talk to. Actors, especially the Hollywood variety, are generally so boring, so derivative, so unsure of who they are. Not so with Jon Lord. He knows exactly who he is and where his band belongs in the pantheon of rock gods. Talk about forthcoming.

On Ian Gillan: "Astonishing voice, but mad as a box of wasps."

On Ritchie Blackmore: "He's a lot nicer than his reputation. He's a pretty good guy… Sitting in front of a log fire with a glass of wine there's no better companion."

On Ray Manzarek: "I love Ray's sound."

On Mick Jagger: "Mick's a chameleon. You never know who you are going to get." On Keith Richards: "a wonderful guy. Have you read his new book?"

On the Beatles: "Didn't they invent everything (in rock music)? And on the seventh day they rested."

On Pete Townsend: "What he did was quite brilliant (Tommy). He took a rock band and played a symphony."

* * *

"It's a pleasure to meet you, sir," Jon Lord says. There are no Willis-like bodyguards. There's no entourage at all.

"The pleasure's all mine," I say. And to myself: Good Lord! When we are seated opposite each other and alone with the door shut, I confess that the riff from My Woman from Tokyo, my favourite Purple song, has been torturing me for days.

"Yeah. That has a nice bluesy riff," he says. He is tall and rather large with long white hair tied back in a ponytail. The courtly Lord looks more like a symphony conductor ready to take up baton than a rock star who invented the quintessential Hammond organ rock sound.

Says Lord: "What you will hear tonight is the mad idea from 41 years ago of putting a rock group inside an orchestra. The concerto. I think that my career in a way was defined by the moment in 1969 when I decided to find out what would happen if you put a rock band in the middle of a symphony…What that did was it opened the door through which many people have since gone and a door that a lot of people might wish we had never opened… That's the first half and in the second half you hear stuff from my solo career and from a certain band I used to be with."

Lord is here to rock the Sala Kongresowa with the Zamosc orchestra, including the Concerto for Group and Orchestra from 1969, which was written for Purple to play with the London Philharmonic. The concerto, which features Ian Gillan's voice, was a milestone at the time and which by chance yours truly had listened to for the first time the day before. It was one of the first collaborations between a rock band and an orchestra although and Ritchie Blackmore and Ian Gillan especially were less than enchanted with the prospect of being tagged as "that group which plays with orchestras." Gillan and Blackmore were keen to create a much harder rock style. But more of that soon.

Lord, who quit touring with the latest purple line-up in 2002, last released a recorded tribute to his great friend, the English writer and barrister John Mortimer, one of Britain's preeminent post- war playwrights. For sheer fun and in typical British fashion these two phenomenal artists toured small venues in the UK with Mortimer's one-man show featuring songs by Lord and sometimes the purple keyboardist himself playing.

How did it happen?

"I did a couple of shows with him, and he said this is going rather well: You wouldn't want to write a couple of pieces? So, I did. And then I suppose about forty times over the following years I did the show with him. When I was ever free. We went up and down the length and breadth of the UK doing the show in church halls and little theatres, and it was wonderful and always a packed audience listening to John, this great raconteur, and quite often people would come up to me and say…"

"Didn't" you used to be with…?"

"Exactly. And I'd say yeah, and they'd say what on earth on you doing here doing this? In a church hall in Nether Wallop. Somewhere in the middle of nowhere."

He is anywhere but nowhere today. He's in Poland, where heavy metal is cult stuff and Deep Purple is the real deal.

"Okay let's go. I have to ask you: do Ritchie Blackmore and Ian Gillan still hate each other?" He did say he wanted to get into trouble.

"Comprehensively," says Lord. "Ritchie always has the belief in his mind that the right singer is lurking behind the bend. And then he gets round the bend and finds the next singer and it's not quite like he thought he would be… Ritchie's always had problems with Ian because he (Ritchie) is a guitarist, and these guys think guitarists rule the world. And God bless them they do. The guitar is the archetype rock instrument. Without the electric guitar we wouldn't have rock music."

Paul Rogers was Blackmore's choice to follow Gillan when he left the band after repeated quarrels with Blackmore.

"Ritchie loves Paul Rogers. They were going to work together when Ian left the band, but Paul of course had the Bad Company thing going… But I really don't think the perfect singer for Ritchie exists.

Where would you rate Blackmore in the history of rock guitarists?

"I rate him very highly," says Lord.

Top ten?

"Most certainly. I think so."

Me: I don't remember where Rolling Stone rated him. (Number 55 as it turns out).

"Well, you see the critics are quite snarky about hard rock," says Lord. "The thing about Purple is that we never received that critical mass of acclaim that for instance Led Zeppelin did. Why? That's a good question. I have an opinion that we were perhaps less consciously concerned with the blues than Zeppelin although there was an element of the blues in our music. That was how I learned to play the Hammond, with the blues…I think also the incredible success of Smoke on the Water harmed us somewhat with the critical elite… Yeah, well there's a reason why the song was so popular. It's a damn good rock song with a killer riff."

"Smoke" was released on their 1972 album Machine Head and still remains far less annoying than that other great learner-guitarist favourite, Stairway to Heaven. Its instantly recognizable central theme is a four-note "blues scale" melody harmonized in parallel fourths. Blackmore's Fender Stratocaster riff combines after several measures with Ian Paice's hi-hat and Lord's rumbling Hammond, then drums and Roger Glover's bass before the start of Ian Gillan's famous vocal with words describing the burning down of the casino in Montreux. The song is Number 4 in the BBC's top twenty greatest riffs after Sweet Child O' Mine, Smells like Teen Spirit and Whole Lotta Love.

Blackmore had no idea what he'd created. In fact, on the original tape box, it's called the Dam Dam song because, as Jon Lord says, the main riff went "Dam dam dam dam dam dam dam dam dam dam dam."

How great was Ian Gillan?

"Astonishing. Inside this tough rock band, we had a very lyrical tenor who was capable of great lyricism. I think he is in chains now to some extent because he's an older man trying to sing the way he used to: I think Ian is almost ashamed that he can't do it anymore."

Was it drugs that made him crazy?

"No. We were a coke, whisky, and beer drinking band. The in-drink in the sixties invented by the Beatles, some say, was Scotch and coke."

How did you get the idea to hook the Hammond into the stack of Marshalls? That kind of changed rock and roll didn't it.

"I had a job on my hands to compete with this beast that was Blackmore. The great thing about Ritchie was that although he is a trained musician, he refused to be restricted by the harmonic considerations of where he might go. So sometimes his solos are way out there… I think that Hendrix was like a light coming on for Ritchie when he first heard him. That must have been an amazing moment for him. Saying oh, wow, of course you can do that…He kept getting louder and louder and stronger and stronger. He's also a lazy guitarist. He loves strict rhythm like on Highway Star but would sometimes stop and go BLAM and let the feedback do the work for him. So, the rhythm would go, and I had to do that. Imagine rhythm keyboard instead of rhythm guitar. Then of course the sound I was getting was not competing with Ritchie. So, I said to our roadie: can we tap out of the amp in the Hammond and go into the Marshalls instead of the Leslie? And several electric shocks later we had it. We were making In Rock at the time."

Did Deep Purple invent heavy metal or was it just an explosion that was going to happen?

"I think various bands came up with strands that became heavy metal. If you like we are kind of the godfathers of heavy metal. But I think Sabbath; if anyone were to be absolutely guilty of inventing heavy metal it would be them."

What was your finest moment?

"I would without hubris be able to say that Made in Japan is the best live album ever made... It's s a band on fire, isn't it? You know what I mean? We were captured on a couple of nights when we were genuinely about as on fire as you can get. Inspired but...yeah, I would be happy to be remembered for putting a Hammond into a rock band."

Really Being There with Phil Niblock

I'm breaking out in a cold sweat. How can music be atonal if it has a tone?

Schoenberg's question. Not mine. But this thought is running—jogging really—through my mind, along with a slight hangover, as I prepare to talk to someone who should know, the highly esteemed Phill Niblock.

Indeed, I'm fortuitously equipped with precisely the kind of dull throbbing pain in the temples that springs to mind when trying to categorize the avant-garde. I'm almost tempted to say, I know what I like when I see and hear it. All kidding aside, how you define the avant-garde. If you could define it, then it wouldn't be avant-garde, would it? (Besides, isn't it the constant modern preoccupation with classifying everything that is behind that dull headache that troubles all those sleeping and waking hours spent sober?)

The celebrated Phill Niblock and Heiner Goebbels are two of the artists appearing at the 54th Warsaw International Festival of Contemporary Music. The festival features "music that does not focus exclusively on itself but opens on the surrounding world, commenting on it and attempting to change it."

More cold sweat. And this from a guy who sang boy soprano in Penderecki's Passion of St. Luke.

O Crux! Indeed.

But as we say in English, let's get to the crux, the heart of the matter.

This year's performances will highlight contemporary social and political issues including child soldiers in Africa and human trafficking as well as less terrifying, yet determinedly relevant, topics such as the phenomenon of leisure time in modern culture and combating barbarism and cynicism through art in the 21st century. There will also be a series of orchestral and piano concerts including a first-ever performance of Andrzej Krzanowki's Symphony No. 1 (1975). And, yes, there will be a soupcon of Stockhausen, as the critics gingerly say.

The affable and engaging Mr. Niblock will be presenting The Movement of People Working, a concert-installation using electronic sound and three video screens, while Mr. Goebbel's contribution will be Songs of Wars That I Have Seen with a text by Gertrude Stein accompanied by the London Sinfonietta. Both productions have won acclaim from critics.

But what does it all mean? Both Niblock and Goebbels would tend to say, "That's up to you."

And they would be right.

This may sound evasive but with both artists, critics and audiences tend to go with the flow, seeking their own personal connection and sense of purpose. Both artists defy classification and intend to keep things that way. And perhaps that is a good thing in a world gone mad with the instant gratification of neat classification. In Lady Gaga Land, where total nonsense is treated seriously in order to roll out the big bucks and where even the Rolling Stones, the Beach Boys and Beatles (Hell the Sex Pistols!) have started to look positively Mozartian, a dose of the abstruse may be just the antidote. I'll leave it to you.

While Goebbels' work weaves its way between the three conventions of opera, theatre and orchestra, Niblock's metier is video accompanied by minimalist shifts in musical tone which suggest an audible version of the earth's hum, which scientists have recently [???]. But more of Mr. Goebbels, who was unavailable for interview at press time, later... Phill Niblock was born in Anderson, Indiana, a city of 75,000 near Indianapolis, which was dominated by General Motors when he was growing up. Both his father, an engineer, and his grandfather, a labourer, worked at GM, but "I escaped," says Phill. After leaving the army in 1958, he moved from Indiana to New York, where he worked as a photographer and filmmaker, focusing particularly on jazz musicians including the inimitable Sun Ra and his "Arkestra." He even used to run into Moondog, the blind and legendary street musician, who dressed as the Viking of Sixth Avenue, who was an influence on minimalists like Philip Glass and Steve Reich at Julliard. Moondog was the man. Even Janis Joplin covered one of his songs.

"I never got into Moondog," Phill Niblock says to me.

Hey, wait a minute! The avant-garde, just like civilian life, is a minefield. So be it.

In the early seventies, Phill began filming The Movement of People Working in mostly rural settings across the world including Japan, China, Brazil, Portugal, Lesotho, Puerto Rico, Hong Kong, the Arctic, Mexico, Hungary, the Adirondacks, and Peru. The films show everyday people doing everyday work—particularly their hands and bodies. He shoots only countryside material, nothing industrial. The films go from coastal sands to the high mountains. The sound is up to the perceiver. The film material, too, is quite neutral. There is no attempt to look at personality. You rarely see faces.

Whatever the locale, these vivid films use long takes in high resolution to catch the movement of human beings doing manual labour. There is no contextual meaning, Phill says. Music and video combine in varying simplicity to create empathy with the rhythm and form of the human hands in motion. They are amazing, especially in a world where Carpal tunnel syndrome is more common than a callous. For example, the foundations of marshy St. Petersburg were built on millions and millions of handfuls of clay carried by slaves.

Cut to today.

It's Sunday midday in July when I Skype Phill, who is basking in the sunlight of Calabria, recovering from last night's performance and the wine that followed. In Warsaw the heavens have opened, and the rain is pouring down. Like a monsoon. It's as dark as Italy must be light.

"So how are you doing today after last night's performance?"

"Slightly hungover," says Phill, who is always present on stage at his computer guiding the show.

He has to be present for the thing to happen. The music is played from recorded digital files.

"That's great. Me too," I say, relieved. "So where exactly are you?"

"I'm in the soul of Italy. That's the ball of the foot, where the most weight is carried."

First, a disclaimer, even though I'm looking forward to seeing your show, I'm not sure I have a clue about what minimalism really is. I'm a rock and roller, a blues guy."

"That explains the hangover," says Phill.

"What about yours?"

"Too much good wine," he says.

"Anyway, it's a pleasure to talk to you. Have you ever been to Poland, or should I ask how many times?"

Phill laughs. "My first time was 1985. That was of course a very different time. I came to see Krzysztof Knittel. He was very involved in Solidarity and doing some really underground stuff to support the movement... It was a fantastic time...He was the only real contact I had in Poland.. . I drove in and parked my car and did a concert in a secret location."

The Movement of People Working is his magnum opus, if you will. But how was it inspired? "I guess it was inspired by my being tired of photographing dance. I had worked from the mid- sixties until mid-seventies at Judson Dance Theatre as resident cinematographer...Eventually, I wanted to do something I could handle alone...The natural movement of people is much more interesting than the artificial movement of dance."

"What will we see in Warsaw?"

"I normally show more than one film and as many as six at one performance. The longest are two hours. We will show three in Warsaw, most likely China from '88, Japan from '89 and maybe Brazil or Mexico. We will use four-meter screens in Warsaw, but the size varies depending on the venue. We did a show in September in Milan that had six five-meter screens."

"Is there any overwhelming theme you want to convey?"

"It's political," says Phill. "I don't like to define it. Some people see it as socialist. I see it as people doing hard work."

It may be political but it's also uncannily topical. The Japan film was shot 22 years ago in the exact area where the tsunami struck in March.

Phill Niblock may live mostly in a world entirely of his own making, but he is very much concentrated on the outside world. Yet, he doesn't watch TV. He doesn't read newspapers and magazines, nor listen to radio or popular music...

No TV?

"I don't see TV as art," he says. "The news is disposable. Oh, every couple of months I buy a copy of the International Herald Tribune," he says. "I don't ever watch movies...People send me things, but I don't watch. I do listen to music because I can do that while I'm editing. I don't want to spend time watching TV and films. I'd rather work than watch."

"So, you are the opposite of Peter Sellers in Being There? You are more about really being there."

He laughs again. At 77, he stays as busy as ever. He produces performance and visual art events in New York and Ghent. He has been touring eight months of the year since 1997. His next big project is a new orchestra piece being done in Prague, then a festival in Milan.

One last question: why the focus on hands instead of faces?

"Hands express a lot about people, especially in Italy," he says with a chuckle. Indeed.

Then there is the intriguing Mr. Goebbels, who walks the tightrope of the avant-garde. Roll up for the magical mystery tour because "Songs of Wars I Have Seen," is one of the more conjured and mysterious trips one can take in a concert hall.

Goebbels' composition takes both title and text from Gertrude Stein's 1945 Paris memoir, "Wars I Have Seen," which premiered at the Southbank Hall in London in 2007. Anyone familiar with Stein's work will know that though she was tutor to Hemingway in the 1920s, her writing was often purposely nonsensical, perhaps the word equivalent of atonal music. Perhaps. She did come up with some seminal catch-phrases including "a rose is a rose is a rose," her prime example of how to write about things as they are without describing the way they are.

Goebbels' stage consists of two parts, the foreground "living room" in which female instrumentalists sit; behind them is a group of male wind players and percussionists in black dress. The "songs," are said without emotion by the female instrumentalists, except for one piece spoken by the male percussionist. The setting suggests women commenting on war while men make the big noises. The music includes 18th century orchestral music, techno-electronics, and a trumpet solo over the ringing of Tibetan prayer bowls. Notwithstanding this, the piece has something of the feel of Thelonious Monk on acid about it.

Goebbels drew early inspiration from Eisler, a Schoenberg disciple and long-time collaborator with Brecht. Despite being influenced by the Beatles and the Beach Boys as a teenager, which he played every day at the piano, he's known for valuing a mixture of styles, his trademark, including classical music, jazz, and rock, whilst composing music for theatre, film, and ballet.

His work, even that of his eighties rock band, Cassiber, is undeniably unforgettable. Some of Cassiber, for example, Start the Show and A Screaming Comes Across the Sky, off his A Face We All Know CD, sound something like the great Captain Beefheart played backwards, which definitely is special.

Both artists are sincere in their rejection of mainstream artistic and political values. Both are truly committed not just to being there, to filling space, but to challenging the freeway of popular culture by taking the scenic view of the abyss from the high road. Nothing wrong with that. Both are determined to find a way of really being there. That doesn't sound just high-toned. It sounds, dare I say it, revolutionary.

Or at the very least, evolutionary.

And now I'm going to go soak my head in a tub of ice-cubes. See you at the festival.

Bruce Willis: Still Lazy After All Those Years

Bruce Willis was in fine form, fit, hairless and raring to go, as he arrived in town to promote his latest starring role as spokesman for Sobieski, a spirited take on the vodka genre. Willis was all smiles as he jokingly admits to how his world has been turned upside down ever since he discovered "truth in vodka," the Sobieski catchphrase.

The relatively fresh relationship with Sobieski, the leading Polish vodka brand in the US, began soon after the long-suffering superstar met and then-married lingerie model Emma Hemming in March 2008 at his villa in the Turks and Caicos.

Willis was jet-lagged yet civil as he held court in the Warsaw Bristol Hotel looking oddly like a cross between Michael Stipe and John Malkovich, his co-star in his next film, Red. Willis will portray Frank Moses in Red— "He's got time to kill" reads the tag line—an adaption of the DC comic book mini-series.

Is the film any good?

"It's great. It's huge. A lot of great actors in it: Morgan Freeman, Helen Mirren, John Malkovich. And it's an interesting mix of romance, action and comedy. We'll see how it looks. I haven't seen a cut of it yet. I think it comes out in October."

That sounds like bullshit. Nevertheless, the film also has a series of smaller roles filled by actors like Richard Dreyfuss, Mary-Louise Parker, Brian Cox and Ernest Borgnine.

One has to hope Red is better than Willis's last vehicle, Cop Out, the most puzzling film of 2010. So, how's life?

"I feel like my world is a much happier and better place now," says Willis. "I met and married a wonderful woman and it's made a big difference in my life, something I didn't expect... For much of the last 10 years I was single and unhappy. Now I'm happy all the time."

It's easy, I'm thinking, to see how his co-star in Moonlighting, Cybill Shepard, hated him. He's annoying as hell.

Sobieski marks a departure of sorts for Willis as he goes all out playing himself, a Hollywood superstar as vodka promoter. It's a departure for sure for the once AA-attending, self-avowed teetotaller. Perhaps he lost a packet with Madoff. Perhaps he's struggling to find a way to pay for his daughter Scout's very expensive education at Brown ($50,000 per year).

Who can say?

Is it every boy's dream to be part-owner of a renowned liquor company?

"I've been living the dream for 28 years," he said.

Willis, who turned 55 last spring, was born in Idar-Oberstein, Germany, to an American GI father and German mother, and later raised in the working-class town of Penn's Grove, New Jersey. He turned to acting when he discovered that it could help him to overcome a terrible stutter that he suffered from as a teenager. Taunting he endured as a teen caused him to become a class clown; he used humour as a way of deflecting attention from himself.

"I had to learn how to defend myself as a kid. I had a terrible stutter from around the time I was nine until I was about 17 and it could make life very difficult if you let other kids tease you and push you around. So, I had to take care of myself when the occasion demanded. You learn not to take shit from anyone. But basically, I learned to make friends with humour and making faces and doing things to make people laugh. I figured out that if I could make the other kids laugh the they wouldn't care about my stutter. I even got elected student council president, which is a big thing in high school."

After employment as a security guard and private detective, he enrolled in theatre school at Montclair State University. Willis first found fame of sorts as a star bartender in Manhattan and studied acting with Stella Adler, which eventually led to several auditions and his breakthrough role in TV's acclaimed 80s series Moonlighting.

Rumours have it that he was pretty wild back then. You can still meet people in Los Angeles and New York who remembers the young Willis's wild ways.

"I spent a lot of time tending bar in New York, and I had the time of my life. It's that part of your life in your twenties when you're kind of fearless and wild and you feel very free. So, New York will always be a huge part of who I am," he says. "I probably had as much fun as any guy could have who is single and likes to party with good friends. I met so many interesting people in New York and before I started getting acting jobs, I was perfectly happy with my life as a bartender. I was making good money for a working-class kid from New Jersey and honestly, I felt like I had the world at my feet. Even when I started making big films and earning more money than you could ever dream of it didn't make me feel any happier or more satisfied than what I had before. It put things in perspective for me."

So, is it hard being a superstar? Can he walk past a mirror?

"I don't pay too much attention to it. My experience with it is very different than yours would be. I don't take it very seriously. I take my work as any actor seriously, but the fame part is impossible to take seriously. I go on shows like Letterman to make fun of myself and he helps a lot. We always have a good time."

What's the secret to your success?

"Let's see now…Seriously, what's funny is that I always believed that I was going to make it as an actor. I told myself that if I stuck to my dream and I believed in myself that eventually I would make it big. Maybe that was arrogant or naïve, I don't know. But if you don't have a little arrogance or a little swagger in this business, you don't have a chance. There's too much competition and too many people telling you you're never going to make it. So, if I meet someone who doubts themselves, I just tell them to suck it up and don't let anyone mess with their dream."

The first Die Hard film in 1988 made Willis emerge as one of Hollywood's leading superstars, a megastar as late-night talk show host David Letterman says. His personal life also became the subject of intense scrutiny during the course his highly-publicized 13-year marriage to actress Demi Moore, which ended in 2000 and produced three daughters, Rumer, 21, an actress; Scout, 18, soon entering her second year at Brown University, and Tallulah, 16.

Willis, who made being bald cool as Butch in Pulp fiction, and Moore remain good friends despite her marriage to the much younger and taller Ashton Kutcher. Willis has famously accompanied Moore and the wavy-haired Kutcher on skiing trips with their three daughters. He loves skiing and diving. To keep in shape, he still works out three times a week, but has never boxed or done martial arts. Somehow, you'd expect more from John McClane, but that's cool. It is.

An action man must lead an active life. What is Willis' take on his iconic action creation?

"I drew a lot on my own attitudes and sensibilities. We both share a healthy disrespect for authority and a gallows sense of humour. John McClane loves his family first and truth second. He has zero tolerance for anyone that tries to put innocent people in harm's way, and he'll sacrifice his own life, if necessary, to keep that from happening."

Is that similar to your personal code in real life?

"Sure, in a sense. I would do anything to defend my family and I have always made my daughters the highest priority in my life. I have tried to be the best father possible to them and I think they're turning out pretty well. And they have a great mother also to help guide them in life.

"You can't predict chemistry. You never know." He famously quarrelled consistently with Cybill Shepherd on the set of the comedy Moonlighting and has publicly shown his displeasure with her as recently as the last couple of years, even though she once called him "a modern-day Cary Grant."

Is he?

"I'm just the modern Bruce Willis...I'm happy with that. I am in great spirits. I'm the happiest I've ever been, and this comes after a long period of being kind of lonely even though I tried to convince myself that I was enjoying my life."

Does he have any regrets?

"None at all. I just saw that there's no point to living with regret or antagonism or having any pent- up anger. You have to let it all go. It was a tough time for me during those years after my marriage broke up. But I had a long talk with Will Smith one day and he kind of explained to me how I had to make an effort to be good friends with Demi for the sake of our girls and how they would have a much happier life and feel so much better if their mom and dad could stay friends and still be happy spending time together even if they had moved on with their lives. That was a great decision in my life and to tell you the truth it's worked out really well."

Will the conquering hero fall in love with Poland as Napoleon did before him?

"Hard to say, hard to say," Willis says with a smile. "Warsaw's a great town, great people. I'll be back. I have to come back for the rye harvest in October."

I don't know about you, dear reader, but I think I need a drink. Interviewing a Hollywood star can suck big time.

Scott Schulman: A Dedicated Follower of Fashion

"**F**ashion embraces the abstract. Designers create a little world every season from head to toe, a full look, shoes, bags, dresses while street fashion is what people are really wearing. The runway shows are much more abstract than what ends up on people. That is much more real to me..." Scott Schulman

Big Blogger

Let me say at the outset, that I hate the word blog. It sounds like a disease or some terrifying event as in:

"I have some bad news for you, sir. We are going to have to remove your blog." Or: "In medieval times Blog ravaged wholes kingdoms and was responsible for millions of deaths. Or: "I got blogged yesterday by some skinheads."

Or a sci-fi movie from the sixties starring Steve McQueen: The Blog!

That aside, ugly as the word is, blog and blogging are here to stay. And some people are simply geniuses at blogging, like today's subject. Are you sitting comfortably? Then we can begin.

Is fashion blogger Scott Schulman (thesartorialist.com), the most powerful commentator in the fashion business? Maybe. His CV is impressive: columnist for GQ, high-profile campaigns for Burberry and DKNY Jeans, a best-selling book, and a place on TIME magazine's 2007 list of Top 100 Design Influencers. Scott Schuman is the street-style blogger who paved the way for the many others who have followed in his original footsteps.

However, if not the most powerful, he may well be the most vertically challenged man in a business whose money is built on appearances, is ruled over by massive egos and whose wares are portrayed by exasperatingly airheaded, infuriatingly elongated models. In short, Mr. Schulman is short. T.E. Lawrence short. Mr. Schulman also uncannily resembles the legend of Arabia. Yes, he is a man of modest height and manner and of immodest achievement: the first millionaire blogger in a very bitchy business.

Yes, Mr. Schuman is short. There! I said it! That's cool. I'm not suggesting he has a Napoleon complex. He seems a thoroughly nice chap. But I am suggesting that his stature—way south of Cruise-height—is an at once startling visual fact that everyone in this most superficial of enterprises seems to refuse to address. It's probably not a conspiracy, but it may be the most closely guarded secret since the Manhattan Project. I could find no mention of his height and very little about his own stylish looks anywhere in any article.

Weird.

Though there is this very cool website in which short celebrity is… well…celebrated: see fuckyeahshortguys.tumblr.com where five feet, four inches tops. (163 cm.)

Suffice to say, he and Madonna can see eye to eye. Literally, if not figuratively. And you have to love it. Here's why: Scott Schuman is the living embodiment of passive- aggressive rebellion against the fashionistas—this mild-mannered Midwesterner from Indiana whose heroes are Mom and Dad, Picasso, Tony Randall (the actor who played Felix in the Odd Couple on TV), and the designers of the Apple Mac. Our hero.

His blog took off because, as he puts it: "I shot things that people would aspire to. Think it took off not because I was shooting the incredibly different, but because I was shooting something people could relate to, a lot of different people could relate to and I don't think there was one time, one particular thing that made me say 'this is really becoming popular.'"

Potentate of taste or not, Mr. Schulman is an interesting guy with an original and attractively simple outlook. He takes photos of regular street folk who appeal to him with their style. He's hooked. He's a street-style junkie cruising corners looking for eye candy.

In 2005, after 15 years in fashion sales and marketing, he took out his camera, started a website and revolutionized the e-spacey world of fashion with down-to-earth style. Thanks very much. His work is an epitome of style over fashion, which is "more abstract."

And style is where's it's at. Keith Richards has style. Lady Gaga has fashion. Style is wearing clothes effortlessly. Fashion is contriving a style, trying to impress. Fashion is turning up at all the latest places saying, 'look at me'. Style is finding a place you like and making it your own. And this is what Mr Schuman is all about.

He says that the simplicity and the interaction with the audience were the two things that made blogging most attractive. "I had an idea for The Sartorialist, this idea of mixing photographs of guys that I knew were stylish with guys that I knew were fashionable, which are two different things, but I only really knew about websites at that time and I knew that a website would take too much time, too many other people would have to be involved and when I happened to be going through the internet I found a blog, just happened to click onto a blog and I'm the kind of person that once I see something interesting I just start hitting all the buttons trying to figure out how they're doing it and it was an interior design blog actually and I thought it was pretty cool."

* * *

Fashion might be the world's third oldest profession after prostitution and spying. (See Raquel Welch in her leopard-skin bikini in the movie 1,000,000 BC.) This is not a criticism. But they just make shit up. You know those crazy catwalk outfits that no one would ever wear, the adolescent sizing of the garments, the starving models. Fashion has not done a good job of representing reality, at least since Twiggy popularized the famine look in the mid-sixties.

Enter Scott Schuman.

Schuman's influence is felt far beyond the internet. He travels the world taking street shots. He is the Henry Rollins of style. Endlessly curious. The first thing he did upon landing in Poznan was to go and snap some photos in the last light of day.

Milan is his favourite destination because of the formality of the style. The old guys still get dressed up every day. He looks for the extraordinary in the ordinary. His photos feature fashion insiders and football fans alike, have been required study in design studios around the world. His photographic style has inspired serious amounts of advertising campaigns and editorials.

* * *

Fashion is ephemeral, style eternal.

"The difference between fashion and style is that fashion is the sometimes stuff. What's happening at that moment? Where style I think is something that's always there in your personal wardrobe. Everybody's version of style is totally different and that's what I think keeps me going out on the street every day, is going out and kind of seeing the variations and what things maybe I'd never seen quite that way that I find very curious and how people will be able to communicate their own persona through their clothing, their posture, the way they wear their hair. I think those entire elements end up becoming very interesting because I don't think I'm really particularly a people person. So, for me I think it's interesting to kind of be able to read people in that way."

What's stylish in the USA?

"In America there are a million different styles: rocker and vintage and sporty and preppy and so I like that variation, so one without the other is not nearly as interesting. All these styles exist together. Then there are the overrated like almost everyone in Hollywood, almost everyone in the record business. But really, I'm just not judgmental that way and I think that sincerity comes through in the blog. I mean to me it really doesn't matter who they are. It's not that I don't want

to shoot people in Hollywood, or models or musicians. If I ran into 20 musicians in a row and they looked great I'd shoot them, but that just rarely ever happens. I don't really fall into that, but for me it's much, much more abstract"

So, what stops him dead in his tracks on the street?

"It's usually much more undefined and it might be a detail. It might be colour combination. It could be even the posture of a girl. Or even the guys. I know a lot of the designers take a lot of those old-guy pictures I take, these kind of really stylish old guys, and I know it's not because of the specific clothes that they're wearing, but it's the posture and it's the attitude and it's the elegance of these guys that is attracting them, that inspires them and it's the same thing for me. I'm totally inspired."

Posture. Attitude. Elegance. Not the label.

So, what would he say about yours truly and my style? I'm wearing a black linen long-sleeved shirt made for me in Nicaragua, old Levis boot-cut jeans, battered Chelsea boots from Timberland, an old suede three-buttoned jacket, several well-placed beers and a twisted smile.

"I would say that you are a regular guy with a bohemian/artistic thing going on," says Scott. "Right on, baby."

Does he have a shooting routine?

"It's pretty random. When I'm shooting, I try and keep it just very easy, very unplanned. I'm just walking around on the street looking for somebody that I think looks cool and I might be able to get a good shot. That is why it's fun. That's why I enjoy going out and getting lost hopefully every day or every other day and just seeing what is out there because by the end of the day I usually get back to my office and think I never would have thought I'd run into that kind of person there doing that thing and by constantly challenging myself that's what I think keeps the sincerity of the blog."

Blogging can be romantic. Scott met his girlfriend online. Find her at GaranceDore.fr.

"It's not just because she is my girlfriend, but I do truly think that she has got the best women's fashion blog in the world. Her point of view is great. Her writing is great. Her photography is great. The way that she communicates is brilliant. The way she writes and the ability to be that stylish and that fashionable and yet that approachable. It's a real challenge to be able to do that and do it consistently every day because you can't fake it."

How important are fashion magazines these days versus the internet?

"You know I'm a self-taught photographer and I taught myself photography just looking, looking, looking at the magazines, so to be honest a lot of them I hardly ever read. I don't really look at what their real fashion opinion is. For me it's always been very abstract, so I don't know. I can't really… I love my fashion magazines. I think I look at them less now just because I've started to develop my own photographic style that I'm very comfortable with, but they really are the ones that taught me the idea of how I wanted to shoot."

What kind of tips can you offer to aspiring amateurs?

Shoot from the heart, that's a good one. I think I'll actually just stop at that. Shoot from the heart I think would be the best. I don't shoot just all young hipsters. I shoot old and young, and that brand comes across in the variety of people I shoot because I actually have something to say, and I can do that as opposed to saying one thing over and over. It gives me a wider vocabulary to be able to shoot people in a lot of different ways and a lot of different types of people, but you always know it's one of my shots and that's because I take it very seriously and I have a real passion about it. I have a real point of view. That's what someone has to do before just deciding to go out and take pictures of people in the street. They really have to have a point of view. You know it's very important what I don't shoot as opposed to what I do shoot. Without a real passionate point of view, I don't think there is anything to do because then it just becomes a report on a product. There are a lot of blogs like that, and I think they're incredibly boring. Just showing what is out there doesn't do anything for me."

What really makes a photo special?

"I don't know. You can't really do anything. I mean at least for me anyway because it's so many different things. I mean it's the clothes themselves. It's the person. It's I just have to... You know that's the artist. But real elements of design are always a good place to start."

Richard Horowitz: A Unique Way of Seeing

It's been a weird ride... starting two days earlier with Janiak, my editor and well-known sophisticate, calling me to do an interview with Ryszard Horowitz. When I heard the name Horowitz I Immediately said yes. I needed the money. My exchequer was lower than a desert wood rat's derriere in Death Valley.

"How much," I snapped.

Olivier said: "More than you deserve, but I have no choice. All my decent writers are busy." "That's my price," I said.

"You'll go down to Lodz on Saturday morning with Marta. Try not to get too drunk the night before."

"Anything you say, boss," I lied.

Marta is a voluptuous blonde who combines the provincial good looks of Princess Diana in her prime and the chutzpah of a young Annie Leibovitz, only taller.

On Saturday morning there we were, whirring toward Lodz in a Smart car, wind in our hair and knees in our face. To get the full experience you had to be there.

Two hours later we rolled up in front of the ancient vodka factory on the outskirts of David Lynch's favourite Polish town. Lodz! That town whose name is absolutely impossible to pronounce properly at first glance unless you are Polish. You see the Poles have this special L with a line (oblique) through it that they like to pronounce like a W so that Lodz, in English phonetics actually becomes Wooch.

Never mind.

Here's a little background on Mr Horowitz (who certainly deserves better treatment than this after what he has been through).

Richard Horowitz was born in Krakow in Poland on May 5th, 1939, several months before the German attack on Poland. His family was on Schindler's List and Richard is one of the youngest known survivors of Auschwitz. In 1959, after studying at the Academy of Fine Art in Krakow, he moved to New York to attend the Pratt Institute and became a New Yorker. His close circle of Polish friends in the 1960s included Roman Polanski, a companion from childhood, film producer Gene Godowsky, writer Jersey Kolinsky, violinist Michal Urbaniak, vocalist Urszula Dudziak and so forth. All of them pre-eminent in their art.

Richard chose photography, his lifelong passion. From the beginning, his work caught fire. He was a force to be reckoned with. His work has been shown, published and collected around the globe. He has been awarded every major accolade a photographer can receive. Most of all he is recognized as a pioneer of special effects photography, the precursor of digital imaging.

Here is what the author of Schindler's List had to say to Ryszard on his 70th birthday.

Dear Ryszard,

Greetings. I had a change of address, and your dazzling book has just reached me. Like your earlier one, which I still cherish and possess, this one is wonderful to look at—as you must yourself know. To me, a mere punter as they say down here in the Antipodes, it's so conceptually exciting to me, and the creativity seems so easy that I wonder why everyone can't let their brain fly as you do. It's because the rest of us aren't Horowitz, that's why.

Ryszard, I can't but look at these knockout images without thinking of your early history. In a sense neither can you, since I see you address it at the end of the book.

It's my guess that after those beginnings and wounds, of the kind no earthly child should bear, you must not always—in the watches of the night—feel as lustrous and celebratory as your images are.

It's easy for me to say, but this makes the light-filled, affirmative images all the more a miracle. The shadow of the KL doesn't seem to fall across your colour-filled, mentally sportive, cosmically and joyfully declarative work at all.

It shows how fierce in you burned the fires of life over those of ... well, I'm sure you don't want to be reminded by a stumbler from Oz.

May I add my congratulations to the worlds, and thank you again for seeking me out in my Australian fastness."

Tom Keneally
(The Author of "Schindler's List")

August 2013. Summertime and the livin' is easy…as Gershwin wrote. Capitol Hill in the District of Columbia is nice this time of year. Congress is in recess. In late August the weather is hot and sunny every day, and you realize what a green and accommodating city the capital really is. The museums are free. The phalanx of joggers perspires. Tourists wander.

All seems well… But there is trouble! Hurricanes on the horizon! Look east, way east. Syria. Assad's boys used poison gas. What? These guys never learn. Picture Assad measuring himself for a Sadat-type hole in the ground… It's a mixed bag. It's anybody's guess what will happen at this point. September 1. Secretary of State Kerry compares Assad to Hitler. This is exactly the kind of rabble-rousing that Kerry deplored when he ran against Bush in 2004.

I slap myself in the forehead. Wait a second! Are those sneaky buggers about to invade Poland? Note to self: cut down on the margarita intake.

* * *

A month earlier, I woke up in Warsaw and turned on the computer.

It's 7 a.m. and I have to catch a ride to Lodz to meet Ryszard Horowitz. I'm scanning Yahoo main page and my eye zeroes in on a fresh item. One of Schindler's actual lists is up for auction in Australia. Kismet. On the way down in the car, we're listening to Michael Jackson's Greatest Hits—music I never listen to voluntarily—and I'm thinking about Quincy Jones (who produced Thriller and started out in jazz in the fifties). Ryszard (Richard?) started out photographing Dave Brubeck, Louis Armstrong, Thelonious Monk, Ella, haunting the night clubs of New York where he landed in 1959 as a student at the Pratt Institute, trading grey totalitarian Poland for the bright lights of the Big City, the capital of photography, New York.

Three hours later I'm talking with the estimable Mr Horowitz at the old Polmos factory in Lodz. He is there to shoot a series of photos for a company calendar. It's a gig. He likes to work. It's been a long time since

I met him at a cocktail party at Gene Gutowski's house in Warsaw. That must have been 1993 or 94 when Spielberg was making the Schindler movie in Krakow and I, the kid from London, was writing a treatment for MGM with Gene.

Ryszard (Richard)? reminds me immediately of Noam Chomsky, the noted MIT linguist and polemicist. He's a dead ringer for Chomsky. Even his voice is similar, soft and thoughtful, the calm eyes masking a ready sense of humour. He is one of the most remarkable people you could ever hope to meet. He is not only a living historical icon, but he is one of the most accomplished photographers of the 20thth Century. And at 72, he is still working! He didn't give it all up to become a real estate developer, he says.

* * *

Rewind. January 1945. The liberation of Auschwitz-Birkenau Death camp. The Nazis had murdered 1.1 million people, by the most conservative estimates, in Auschwitz alone. Hitler and his gang of cutthroats had perfected torture on an unimaginable scale. Russian troops liberated the remaining prisoners, including the five-year-old Ryszard Horowitz. Released into the company of nuns, he was soon reunited with his mother, and they moved in with Roman Polanski and his aunt. Jews were in short supply, and they had to stick together. These two children would mature into epitomes of their professions. Extraordinary.

The question comes to mind: how you talk to someone whose experience is so awesome, so beyond your own. Well, you just talk, you just listen.

Right now, today, he's doing a calendar using the vodka factory as a background. "It's very exciting, he says, eyes sparkling. "What I did was to combine this dilapidated building with gorgeous looking girls. So, I had a very large crew working with me. We brought in movie lights … They were very helpful and left me pretty much alone and now I have to prepare all these images to get 12 of them… It appears that they pay great attention to the quality. So, let's keep our fingers crossed it comes out as I see it."

Ryszard is a New Yorker, but he keeps in touch with Poland. He visits twice a year, usually to pick up some award he's being presented with.

He laughs.

"Yes, you've won a lot of awards," I say. "I'm in the wrong field. You just have to show up in your field, and they start hanging medals round your neck. You started winning stuff right away in 1963, didn't you?"

"Yes, that's right," he says, laughing. "Yeah, yeah, yeah, yeah. Makes my kids proud of their daddy. He's working on his autobiography now.

"You know my life was divided into two stages, war time and Poland until I left, and then the rest of my life in the States. The connecting point is the art education I received here. I graduated from the high school of fine art in Krakow and then attended the Academy of Fine Art in Krakow. And then I got a scholarship at the Pratt Institute in Brooklyn. That is how my so-called career started."

It was hard leaving Poland. He was going from the quintessential grey communist state, the Hungary Rising recent, to the glittering lights of New York.

"I did have a wonderful group of people I grew up with in Krakow, many of whom made great careers. And then the juxtaposition between Poland at that time and America. No colour and no light and a hard life! Then things were happening in New York... The sixties were a quite wonderful time. I was very fortunate to be at Pratt then. I met some great art directors and graphic designers.

And some of them offered me work with their companies."

He started off as a photographer, obsessed with portraits of the jazz greats of the time —he'd met Dave Brubeck in Poland, was friends with Komeda. It was a Who's Who. He worked as a graphic designer in TV doing title cards and graphics. He did station breaks. Everything by hand. Everything that was used before, during and after a show.

Through his mentor, Alexey Brodovitch, he met some of his heroes including the great photographer Richard Avedon and Willis Conover, the DJ on Voice of America radio who bombarded Eastern Europe with contraband jazz during the Cold War.

"I grew up with all the so-called legends of jazz and also photographed them. As a matter of fact, a new book just came out called All That Jazz. It was co-written by Dave Brubeck. He was in Poland in 1958, and I happened to photograph him. We met in New York a few years ago, and I showed my black and white negatives to him from that period. He became very excited. And there's a beautiful book printed here in Poland. It won the most beautiful book in Poland this year."

* * *

"Do you know who Quincy Jones is?"

"Sure. I was thinking about him on the way here, while we were listening to Michael Jackson." Ordinarily Quincy Jones would never cross my mind. Noting a slight mystic synchronicity had slipped between reporter and subject.

With great pride I have to show you something..." Ryszard (Richard?) is searching for photos on his iPhone. "At any rate the book was written by George Ween, the creator of the Newport jazz festival, and consists of photos from Poland and the States...Of course, I was fortunate to photograph Armstrong and Ellington and people like that. The book is out and is attracting a lot of interest. Let me just quickly dig out this thing I want to show you...o...(laughs) are you ready?"

"Boy am I!"

"There it is."

"Well, that is Quincy Jones holding the book and giving you a big thumbs up."

"He also wrote me a lovely, very kind of profound letter."

"In what way?"

He was commenting on this whole bizarre situation that jazz is not really appreciated in the States but in Europe and Japan and China people are crazy about jazz and lots of great musicians are forced to leave the States. When I moved to the States you could see all these great musicians in jazz clubs that were almost empty. I remember seeing Ella Fitzgerald in a place with maybe ten other people. This was the early 60s. I also used to go to a place called Five Spot to hear (Thelonious) Monk. I was sitting right next to him and again there were again maybe five people. I went to the first Nancy Wilson concert with Cannonball Adderley the alto sax player and nobody was there!"

"That reminds me of when I play rock and roll. Does that mean...?"

Ryszard (Richard?) Horowitz laughs.

"As a matter of fact, in my book I have a CD attached inside the back cover that has a fabulous video of me with Dave Brubeck at his villa in Connecticut, a beautiful villa he built with the money from Take 5. He comments on my photos and tells a wonderful, wonderful story about how he came to Poland (in the 1950s) and how he was welcome, and people were freaking out. He was the first real jazz musician that we experienced and of course people knew him from Willis Conover's broadcasts. So, he was extremely impressed and despite all his travels throughout the world this trip made a lasting impression. You know he had a true photographic memory. A great talker. He could remember any period, not just this one. So, there is this film and at the end he plays the tune he wrote about Poland called 'Dziekuje.' Which you think would be popular here, but no one knows it. And there is music performed by some of the heroes of my book like Jerry Malligan and Jimmy Rushin and Joe Williams, amazing, amazing, amazing and Count Basie... So, for me one of my main reasons for wanting to go to the States was jazz, apart from wanting to get out of Poland."

"What did jazz represent?"

"Freedom and joy."

"Of course. And who would know better than you? I once had a girlfriend and I asked her what the purpose of life is, and she said suffering. And I said don't try to sell any of that horseshit around here," I say.

Ryszard laughs.

"Or Christian..."

"I'll take the music religion please, not that one," I add.

Says Ryszard: "It never stops amazing me when I go to a jazz concert how happy these guys are when they play, how they smile when someone plays a difficult phrase. They love it. They love what they are doing."

* * *

"Talking kismet now, Ryszard. On the way here the driver was playing a Michael Jackson tape.

And I thought of Quincy Jones. And this morning when I got up—very early—to drive here, I read a fresh story online that one of Schindler's Lists is up for auction. Did you hear about that?" "Oh yes, yes, yes."

"As a person who somehow miraculously survived this—how do you think it has it affected you? I mean Freud said we are formed by the age of seven." (I'm pretty sure that wasn't Freud).

I'm treading on possibly thin ice here, but Ryszard indulges me...

"I'm sure that it affected me inside, but I consider myself to be blessed and fortunate that it did not warp my mind. I know so many survivors who are haunted—to this day. They cannot, even now, enjoy life in any way. They are in despair. They talk about it, they live it...I somehow was able to put it aside and made a conscious effort never to use it to advance my career as a matter of fact, it was only after Spielberg's film was released that people knew about my past. I didn't choose to reveal it. Spielberg did."

"Spielberg outed you!"

"Exactly!"

"He fooled me because he invited me to the shooting of the last scene with the survivors (in Israel). After that I started getting letters, for instance from ancient mistresses that I had forgotten, that I hadn't seen for a long time: 'Oh I wish I had known. It could have been so wonderful blah blah blah...' As far as my work is concerned...it's considered to be very whimsical. To be amusing and to be happy. On the other hand, though, there is a group of people who see dark imagery.

Whenever I show a head with a hand or a leg or something, they say that I am showing body parts. Are you ready for that? He laughs, which is something that would never cross my mind. And I'm sure that some things slip in here and there. Goodness knows we are only who we are, but never in my mind would I dwell on it...Except very recently, I was asked to design a poster for the 70-year anniversary of the Ghetto Uprising. Two eyes with flames coming out... But generally, I don't like to address this issue in my work."

"Did people see that imagery before they knew you were a survivor?"

"No, of course not."

"There's your answer. At any rate we don't seem to really know how our experiences affect us." "That's absolutely true. Unless they are put into a context."

"A frame of reference."

"Sure, sure. Our work doesn't always express our experience."

"Maybe you said somehow, 'forget that shit and move on'."

"Well, there are plenty of artists who latched onto the experience, like Kantor and Szajna. He was a friend of mine. I knew both of them. But Kantor died when I was very young. But also, there is a whole group of graphic artists, even colleagues from the Academy of Fine Arts, who spent the rest of their life printing really horrific, grotesque things that show the worst of human nature, although some of them had not even had first-hand experience...Still, they grew up in this atmosphere. For some people it's a way of healing themselves. I know that once you dwell upon it it's terribly painful. I have a sister who lives in Krakow still, older than me, a survivor as well, and she's much more damaged, quote unquote, psychologically. And she's one of the last witnesses. She was the girl who gave a birthday cake to Schindler, and he got lots of shit about it from the Gestapo..."

"That scene in the movie, right?"

"Yes…But there is also another fascinating detail about Schindler. He was totally unaccepted after the war. He was considered to be a Nazi. And it was virtually forbidden to speak his name out loud!"

"People didn't know?"

"My father describes in great deal his recollection about everything, about everybody but Schindler."

"Why was it so?"

"He was persona non grata… How could father say he was saved by a Nazi? They were branded a certain way. No one would believe what Schindler did, because 99% were savage bastards. But there was also a fraction that was helpful. In our case we were saved also by an SS officer who was a sidekick of Amon Goth, the one who was shooting people from his window. He was a client of my father before the war. He said something to Goth. And because of that I was saved. Because of that I was saved form the most brutal round-up of children. There were hundreds and hundreds of children shipped away from Auschwitz who perished. And I…I was in a group of ten kids who were saved at the time. There is no question that I was saved because of that German officer."

"What was your father doing?"

"He was running one of Schindler's businesses. You know there is a person who was played by Ben Kingsley called Isaac Stern…He was a composite of several people and one of them was my father. He was very close to Schindler and as a matter of fact they met a few times after the war… My father was really very close to Schindler. I want to make a point about how things change. He became a hero in a former communist country but while he (Schindler) was alive, he was totally brushed aside. I honestly had no opportunity to ask my parents why they were afraid to talk about him. My father mentioned briefly that he worked at Schindler's factory and later on moved to another place. As far as I'm concerned, I owe my life to him and a few other people. At the end of the war, I was pulled away from his place to Auschwitz. The last several months of the war I spent there."

"Do you remember anything? What was it like?"

"Oh yes, I remember the end very well. (Laughs) What was it like? It was mud. It was Death. You know, I cannot even talk about fear because we were, you know, psyched up; we were so into it that we didn't know anything different. For me at the time, this was the norm. We were talking about Freud and how you are formed by your early experience… After the war it was very hard for me to get readjusted to normal life.

My sister and my father said I used to hide food and I used to hide things after the war…just to keep things… What else? I remember when we were liberated by the Soviet Army. I remember they took some photographs. As a matter of fact, there are a couple of pictures of me from that period in the camp museum today… My mother learned about my survival when she got out of (another) camp. She didn't know I was alive…and there was a large screen erected in Krakow at the old market square with a documentary movie being shown of the last days of Auschwitz…I'm there with a group of nuns who were taking care of us. And my mother freaked out. She went to the projectionist and begged him to give her a couple of frames of the movie…which I still have…So, she went to the orphanage to find me and what did she find out? That I had been taken away by the aunt of Roman. Roman's aunt! And then we lived together under one roof. That was until 1948, when we moved to another flat. So, I have some flashes of memories, some details. When I look back at photographs of the time, it brings back a lot of memories. Most of the time I was in the pre-verbal stage…so it's hard to even describe these things…So we were one of…maybe the only, family that survived pretty much intact."

How did you come through this?

"What helped me after the war was the fact that I had my parents with me. That's a big difference! Big difference… the warmth you know…"

"And you had Roman and his family."

"That's right and he was scarred as we know. For Roman it was a different situation. Look: he also is a few years older, so he had more memories, so he remembers more."

* * *

It was a gilded age for Poles abroad: they were doing extraordinary things, escaping into fame from the Soviet world. Among them were illustrator turned film producer Gene Gutowski, who produced Polanski's first three films and just missed out doing Rosemary's Baby, celebrated writer Jerzy Kosinski (his celebrated and controversial 1965 novel, The Painted Bird, depicts a boy's brutal experience wandering through Poland during World War II) and cinematographer Adam Hollender, who won an Oscar for Midnight Cowboy in 1969. But Roman Polanski was family.

Now we are riffing like jazz on our own be-bop beat…

"Gene Gutowski is a friend of mine. Did you meet Gene in New York?"

"I met Gene through Roman in London when they were doing Repulsion. I met him later on many times, in New York and then in Warsaw when he moved to Warsaw (in the 90s)."

"What about Kosinski?"

"Kosinski, I knew well. We spent a lot of time together in the 60s, 70s and into the 80s…We did have one big argument."

"What did you argue about? Women?"

"Women! Ha ha! No! He was very possessive guy, and he was very conscious of his image. When he was just about to republish The Painted Bird (in the 80s) he asked me to take a portrait photo of him, which I did, and when I brought the picture to him, he insisted that I leave my negatives with him. He simply wanted to own them. He just wanted to have it. I said, 'No. This is mine.' Whenever you want a print, give me a call and I will make one for you. So that was that. And then later on, we became friends again. Then, when was with Ula, Ursula Dudziak. We spent lots of time together. I saw him several days before his suicide—which was to some extent a shock to us."

"Why did he do it?"

"You see he was ill. Not just psychologically but physically. He had a problem with his blood pressure. He was weak. And he recalled the way his father died, and his father was pretty much disabled. And Kosinski was very physical. He liked skiing and swimming and polo. He was just afraid of becoming a vegetable. I remember we were in a bar in New York with a group of people. It was his birthday, as a matter of fact, and he already talked nonsense. He sorts of hinted to us that he was going to do something with his life. It was not very obvious, but it was frightening. He said, "Maybe I should end it.""

"Did you take him seriously?"

"Well, you always have to take people seriously…but you don't think they will do it. He was also involved with the Hemlock Society. People choosing the way to go…So, the whole thing was peculiar about the way he died and the way he was discovered. There are a lot of question marks about why the police acted the way they did…Anyway, it was a shock to us all. I have my own opinion about his life…but what was remarkable was to have me and Polanski and Kosinski in the same room. Both of those guys wanted to outdo each other and be on the top.

Those are two very strong personalities. They liked each other but then Kosinski made up this story when the Manson tragedy took place. Kosinski was interviewed and he claimed that he was on his way to Roman's house, just about to get on a plane to go there, and had he done it he would have been killed. But this is bullshit. Because I spoke to Roman about this and it's not true."

"Gene was pissed off with Jerzy..."

"Gene was a different thing with Jerzy because he was so protective of Roman."

Ryszard Horowitz has been very forthcoming. Our half-hour meeting has run to over an hour by now and still going strong, but there are photographs to be taken in the dilapidated vodka factory. "Well, this is endlessly fascinating stuff, Ryszard, but as we are running out of time, now comes the moment we've all been waiting for. I've got to ask you about the Horowitz—wait for it...style."

His rich laughter punctuates my question.

"You mean: what is it?"

"I thought you might know," I say.

"I know nothing about it." He is smiling.

"Well, there you are."

"You know it's interesting what people say and what you think yourself. I mean I know I was always outside the mainstream. And it had its ups and downs, but basically, I stuck to my own vision, and I was able to survive with it."

"I think I have to insist on a style at this point," I say.

Horowitz laughs again, but is indulgent, nonetheless.

"No, it's a personal way of seeing things. Some people say there is a certain magic, something surreal...It's the mix of Poland and America. Once a critic called me a Galician surrealist. I retain a lot of soul that is Polish...with American knowhow and with American vision and American freedom. I expanded upon this base... luckily, I managed to get out (of 'communist' Poland) and got a very solid education in Krakow and used it to achieve whatever it is that I have achieved."

"What have been some of your favourite projects besides of course this one here in Lodz? The latest project is always in some way the best, isn't it?"

"Of course, let me see. My big break came when I did some work for Harper's Bazaar (magazine) in its heyday in the late sixties... And that led to my first major campaign for a French company called Rodier.

That was my first big campaign on my own and I used at this time false perspective, when I did things in the camera, when I reversed proportion. And that was very successful, and I thought it would help me in New York and it did to some extent, but it was not the kind of vision that was accepted in America then, but I stuck with it and eventually I got some commercial assignments. Then I became interested in photocomposition, where I assembled images in the darkroom and those images are viewed by people generally as if they were done in Photoshop. People don't know the difference. At any rate, at that time I got a major campaign from Ford, which was fantastic because I had never photographed cars before. I started with jewellery… And this art director from Young and Rubicam spotted those photographs of jewellery and as he told me later on, if I knew how to light a piece of silver, I would be able to light a car… So, I went to California to shoot it and it was a pretty big thing…I shot in Palm Springs and on movie stages in Hollywood. But mostly in California. It was all done in secret…The Lincoln Town car."

"What was your concept?"

"To show cars in a new place. I showed them in different environment, for example a car in the clouds…and I had to learn how to do this…They had me do a car in the jungle a la Rousseau under the moon. This was a breakthrough, and it won any award you can imagine…Then I worked for Tiffany doing more jewellery. I photographed these very precious diamonds…in the water to show the fluidity…And then I did a digital image for Kodak called Allegory. The whole thing was to draw a parallel between what a composer does when he puts strange sounds in harmony. This was an important image because it was the most complex photo image ever made. That must have been the early nineties. And I got criticized for doing something that was not photography. But people came around and we see what happened since then…"

"Yes, so they invented digital imaging to keep up with Horowitz."

"Oh yes. I like the sound of that. Now I'm beginning to like you. Thank you."

"Are we beginning to get along yet?"

"Yes, we are."

"Well…now we'd better go take some photographs of you for this story. All right?"

"Why not? I will show you the factory. It's a wonderful space…"

Jan Kaczmarek: Soundtrack of Life

It's been that kind of summer: shining with synchronicity, plump with atrocity. Full of apocalyptic warnings and ominous invasions! The Euro Cup. Fanatic insanity on a stick, impoverished Spain cheering on its victorious multimillionaire ball-jugglers. Then: Madonna and Romney meet Poland. The Mormon Meets the Kabala. Like some Japanese horror flick. M&M. Sugar-coating with a Nut inside...And: The London Olympics. Yawn! China vs. the USA. More bread and circuses backlit by fiscal chaos. And over there the rat-a-tat-tat as: Batman rises. The Joker takes human form, mowing down an audience at midnight. Syria in flames. Iran in the crosshairs. Etc. Etc. (In July I escaped and dove into Bulgaria like warm oblivion. The Black Sea is green, by the way. And Bulgarians shake their head when they agree. All oddly appropriate, perception being the fickle hussy that she so obviously is.) One wonders: what is exactly the appropriate soundtrack for the cartoon in which we live?

All of the above notwithstanding, on the longest day of the year I found myself dozing lazily, jet-lagged, on a train from Warsaw to Poznan. It's a journey I could do in my sleep (which I did). Jan A. P. Kaczmarek is intimidatingly talented. Super smart. He trained as a lawyer. He studied with Grotowski. Music tempted him for years until passion became profession. Aha! There he is transmitting waves of quietly controlled energy suggesting a super-charged mind burning behind those calm eyes. He is one of the most famous Polish people in the world so getting to meet him is just plain fun. And as Hemingway said, "When you stop doing things for fun you might as well be dead." I couldn't agree more. Jan has won more music awards, including his Oscar for Finding Neverland (2005), than you can shake a stick at. I know this because I hired someone two weeks ago to shake a stick at all those awards, and the stick is still shaking. Try this: Google Jan A. P. Kaczmarek and see for yourself.

Impressive.

His festival: what is it?

Jan says: "Transatlantyk is a festival of ideas. Social conscious-ness is a driving force, illuminated through unique musical and filmic works." There will be artists present. Not celebrities. Talented people. Not big babies preening. That's already an achievement. Thank you very much, Jan.

The interview begins.

"We start just like that?" asks Jan as I switch on my recorder.

"No foreplay," I say. "Straight to business." His assistant giggles. I have the sense that Jan does things for fun. And that puts me at ease, my usual comforting paranoia tucked away for later if needed.

1.

The Transatlantyk Festival is an official partner of the Berlin Film Festival and the Sundance Institute, the model for Jan's idea. It's locat-ed in a palace at Rozbitek, 60km from Poznan. Jan found the place by pure accident. He wanted to do something in Poland and the location between Poznan and Berlin were the perfect fit.

Says Jan: "I wanted a city that is ready for such a thing. And sud-denly we have a freeway that takes only an hour and a half to Berlin. There is also a new airport being constructed by the Germans near our border that will have transatlantic flights. I can fly from LA and have a car pick me up. So, it's very good for us. Poznan is a very good city with a lot of cultural activities, but they doubt themselves somehow. They convinced themselves they had nothing much to offer. It was a big psy-chological defeat when Poznan did not win European cultural capital for 2016. (Wroclaw won.) Poznan didn't even make it to the finals, which to me was ridiculous.

"It must be great to cooperate with Robert Redford. How does that work?"

"Sundance sends five documentaries to us. We have the same teach-ers…The good thing is that documentaries are free from commercial pressure. When you score a feature there is always some level of ex-pectation about how this film will perform at the box office, while with documentaries that element doesn't exist or it's really secondary."

The emphasis is on exchanging perspectives, mostly American and European. Jan is a big fan of American know-how. He has worked with Independents and studios in Europe and America and appreciates both sides of the ocean.

Caveat emptor: this is no Kumbaya hand-holding ceremony here.

"I only have one criticism of Sundance," says Jan. "It's that they take such good care of their participants that it presents an illusion of this world as a paradise, and show business is not a paradise. Maybe we should create a conflict simulation session, so that we don't give the wrong impression."

So: what affects him as a composer?

"Everything affects me. It's a mysterious algorithm mixed with those elements we think we control and with those elements we don't control."

"I write songs. What's the difference between writing songs and orchestrating a movie besides the pain differential?"

"The discipline is the same. It's only a question of practicalities. When you write a song it's enough to have a guitar in your hands, and there you are. When you write for an orchestra you can start with a guitar or often it's a piano, and then you have to think about the other players. With an orchestra you think mostly about the other players. With a song you just play it yourself. There's a chance for a more personal form of expression. In any orchestra there is a chance of disconnection."

(At this point the muzak playing Alice by Smokie—a song that has always made me want personally to throw up on its authors—and Jan gets up to ask the obliging waitress to turn the muzak down.)

"I don't want you to have to hire a special laboratory to extract my voice from the noise on your recorder."

Jan is at the top of his game. He can choose his projects, since he won the Oscar. What's his latest?

"A movie called The Time Being, which is a secret project. I'm not talking about it."

"Don't worry; your secret is safe with me."

"If you know the title you can find out some details."

"I already forgot the title." (The Time Being is about Daniel, a struggling artist who accepts a series of bizarre commissions from a dying, eccentric millionaire (Frank Langella). Daniel can't quite ascertain whether his new "mentor" is a monster who is intent on destroying Daniel's life and marriage, or a saviour who will teach him the true meaning of art.)

"How did you get that job?"

"The director knew some of my work and looked for me and found me."

"They knew you won an Oscar."

"Yes, these days it's hard to hide such things."

"What's it like to win the Oscar?"

"It's a useful title...It's had a very positive effect on my life, and I worked a long time and very hard to get to the top of the profession. So, I don't keep any distance from it. I'm very proud to be the only living Polish composer with an Oscar... It affects your life in sometimes unexpected ways. For me the biggest value is that I've met many interesting people because of the Oscar... My encounters with human beings became something bigger. Instead of meeting 100 people I meet 1000. And then there are the unexpected encounters like someone wants me to help with the promotion of very exclusive champagne, all organic, promoted by Prince Charles to promote the idea of clean organic wine. So, they meet with me, and if I do the music then I get to learn about how to make champagne. So, I get invited into these new worlds and learn new things that I can also put into my work."

"How did you get invited to do your first movie scores?"

There was a young guy just graduated from Lodz film school who knew my ensemble called the Orchestra of the 8th Day OTED in about 1984. And it was a very nice idea. He was influenced a bit by Blade Runner. The imagery ... The film was dangerously mysterious, and the story made no sense but at that time in Poland and in Europe nobody really cared about the story that much.

Only the Americans had the habit of seeing the world as a coherent story. We Poles had the story in our minds and that was enough. We didn't have to put the story on film exactly because it ruined our sense of intellectual adventure (laughter). But seriously speaking, the film was done with limited resources but there was a huge space for music...It was fun... I only did three movies before I left. At that time, I didn't look at film as my future. My music was formed by live concerts and theatre."

And Grotowski?

"I participated in the laboratory, I met Grotowski, but I didn't really know him. It was group therapy... When I went there, I was a depressed former law student, and I needed something different. My next illusion was to be a diplomat. But that was too close to being a KGB agent, a part of the existing bureaucracy. I was cured very fast. I went to Grotowski seeking a solution. I was seeking the purpose of life and in a strange way I found it, because he destroyed me. I couldn't connect any more with the world. I left because again I needed to find something new. I was lucky because a friend gave me a very unique instrument, the citole, a rare version of a zither the German Swiss stringed instrument. So, I got this very rare zither. It was different. It had a small

keyboard but all the sounds were produced by a tremolo and every sound produced by this was so predictable that I couldn't stand it after 30 seconds. So, I removed the keyboard and introduced techniques from other instruments and the most revolutionary was the use of a bow."

The waitress brings Jan's omelette. And more coffee.

Jan says: "We have a very good beginning, so let's stop for a while."

2.

He first started composing at high school in Poznan. Studying piano was boring. He gave it up at 15. He wasn't even sure he liked music anymore. Then the high school theatre was looking for actors. Jan went along. He saw a grand piano standing in the corner and "felt more comfortable going to the piano instead of standing on stage." Slowly he began to riff, to create new music for each performance. He didn't call it composing at first. "The environment was ideal because there was no one to criticize me and everyone supported me. They liked my improvisation. I was watching them and changing the music according to the different emotions at the moment and that seemed unusual."

Then he won a competition to write the school anthem.

"You were the music guy?"

"That's correct… It was only two years, but it seemed like 20. It was so intense. I even had time to found a rock band and then I switched to a jazz trio."

"Why did you switch?"

"Rock was challenging, but I fell under the influence of Michal Urbaniak, who was huge at that point, so I said fuck rock music. I have to do that. I kept disconnecting from mainstream influences. In rock I had all the girls. With jazz much less. Then I went into meditation and kept going from really popular stuff where people could understand me to being less and less understood. Only many years later by moving to

America did I reverse the process and go back to more popular stuff. Anyway, I got a very interesting kind of freedom not belonging to one channel of culture."

"And that was useful in composing film scores, because there are all kinds of moods. There is a huge difference between Get Low (Depression Era Tennessee) and Finding Neverland (Edwardian England).

"Yes, you need to understand genres plus often when I start a movie there are already a few songs there, so you had better be connected and understand what's going on. The songs are usually not of my own choosing since people play with music before they hire the composer. People play with the movie for months in the editing room and sometimes years. You come into the ready project as a composer.

"So, you are like a script doctor perhaps. Only you are a music doctor."

"Yes. People believe that music can bring some mysterious glue to make the movie flow better.

"But with Neverland that was a different process."

"Yes, it was an orchestra score from the beginning. I've never discussed this with a journalist so now maybe it's time to do that. The original song that played as the film ends and the credits roll was a song performed by Elton John. Not a bad song in itself, but in completely the wrong place for this film. So, we had a few test screenings, and then it was a search for something to put there and lucky me I had a one-day recording with Leszek Mozdzer doing piano variations on my theme. At the time my producer didn't understand why I was spending money on this very expensive recording session when I already had all the music. I said I would like to try this. Leszek is a fantastic pianist and I need this for the CD. Since you are so happy with my score give me this one day. And so, they did. The producer was really in love with the score: he forgot about this session. So, when he came with Elton John's song, I took one of the improvisations and put it where the other song was, and it was like a miracle it worked so well. We were happy to see that quite often the audience was sitting during the credits and listening to the piece. That's how you test it—if people don't leave—because usually they go during the credits.

"How much were you inspired by the film?"

"Very much. The subtle beauty of it. In a way it was exotic to me. I was never attracted to the story of Peter Pan before. It's such an Anglo-Saxon thing." We order more black coffee and a second round of omelettes. Meanwhile we discuss the excellent service at the Sheraton—

how different from the old days! —and the state of things in the US. I make the observation that the service in the US is not always good now. There are stress fractures in the psyche of America. People are cracking. We both wonder what recovery means and what price will be paid by the middle class. And then there is the old Transatlantic Gulf between Europe and the US, which still exists even in the digital age.

Jan: "When I speak about the US in Poland, people know nothing. When you see a debate on TV about politics, it's shocking how misunderstood America is. It is either idealized or simplified. What you are saying to me is obvious because I live there. I run a festival which I call the "Festival of Ideas," including political ideas. We try to educate, especially with documentaries. We are bringing the best including Occupy Wall Street and the other latest stuff.

"I love documentaries. I look at everything on the internet—the whole gamut from the fringe conspiracy stuff to the mainstream documentaries. There is an explosion of films on the net over the last few years. How do you decide what is relevant?"

"I have my own channels to find truth," says Jan. "It's very hard to find truth now. Of course, you don't want to get paranoid on any topic but it's a fascinating time because in the old days you couldn't find information. It didn't travel. Now you can't find it because it travels too much. You cannot find the truth because you are being swamped with waves of nonsense or half-truth or even outrageous lies."

3.

"Where do you feel more comfortable, in Poznan or in LA?"

"I feel comfortable when I change places. When I'm in Poland, I sometimes have too much and when I'm in LA I sometimes have too much of it, too. Once you emigrate you belong nowhere. You are hanging somewhere in between. I have two places mostly. It's sometimes too much to manage. I am thinking about simplifying my life."

"Things are complicated. I read somewhere that we create more information in a few days now than existed in the world before 1900."

"Yes, but it's not true really. The information existed but it was just not transported."

(Our fresh omelettes come.)

"If someone bumped their head in the 14th century it wasn't publicized."

"And now, we should take a photo of our omelettes for Facebook."
(Laughter) "Exactly."

"That's true! But in the old days information didn't travel. Let's say someone broke their leg. It never got publicized and now: straight to Facebook."

"Is there any pepper? Must have pepper"

"We must find it. We have an international crisis on our hands."

"Yes, if we don't find it, I will take my shoe off and beat on the table with it (a la Khrushchev in the UN)."

The kindly waitress provides.

"Anyway, we agreed that information was there, but not transported and now we create this ocean of unnecessary information, and we feel compelled to respond to this information. Historically, when you got a letter, you had two weeks to think about it before you write and send it back and everyone was happy if they got it a month later. Nowadays if you don't respond to a text in seven seconds people think you are rude."

"Yes, I get that all the time. Why do we have to supply instant answers? Maybe you are busy right?
We should post this on Facebook."

"Maybe later: our omelettes are destroyed now."

"Very post-postmodern. The time for perfect omelettes is over. We live in a multiverse."

"Ok, let's do it. We need to document this encounter."

Photo taken. Results scary.

"You can tell it's morning and neither of us slept well, and the omelettes are destroyed with different designs."

"This is a collaboration in conceptual art."

"At least we are doing something. We are not bored. Life is birth and death and as many things in between as possible as long as we are not bored."

The waitress interrupts nicely to ask if we want anything else before breakfast is removed. Maybe we want something else like a croissant or some fruit.

"How about an apple?" I say.

"An apple! Exactly!" says Jan.4.

"What challenges do you face with the festival?"

"It requires integrity and responsibility. Take Grotowski. I think he was a genius in his way. And he created something very important in world theatre—his method of using the actor as a naked force. He de-

veloped that. But as a social engineer he was abusive. He was irrespon-
sible. You cannot do things like this today. You cannot engage the minds
of young people, and then walk away. You destroy them."

"It's mind control: a kinder, gentler Jim Jones thing."

"Yes, and that's what he did. And no one held him accountable
because in communist Poland nobody held anybody accountable for
anything really except the government. He could operate freely, and it
was a very forgiving time. But today as you enter the area of altering
consciousness, I like to bring my initiative and experience. I believe
very much in the American spirit. Yet, I see America as a great structure
which is now falling apart."

"Me too. Or at the very least altering beyond recognition," I say.

"I'm glad you agree with me because you probably know much better,
but in my business, the work is incredible. You cannot find it any other
place on the planet than working in film or the field of music. There is
a sustained effort and endless corrections before finally sending it to the
market. That is why American film is winning and dominating the market.
It's unparalleled. Even if you watch a very bad movie sometimes it takes a
day to recover from this overwhelming emotion to discover that was a bad
movie. You don't have that illusion in Europe. People don't care so much
about story here. What I admire about America is that there is always moral
purpose and transformation, and people want to see some kind of growth.
In European movies they quite often contemplate the contemporary situation. Only the movie starts from a bad situation and ends much worse."

"Are you excluding British films?"

"Yes, because they are in the middle…I believe in this conflict between powers (creative and corporate) and that's why I'm doing the festival. That's why I call it Transatlantyk. Because I believe in the creative
power of the transatlantic connection. There is a collision between the
American and the European ways of doing things. And the result is a
much better film and much better music."

"You must see it in your own life." "I spent 20 years in America, so
my Polish software is altered. I'm somebody else now."

"Both of us have software problems."

"That's why I like this conversation. We meet to connect. I don't
like only answering questions from journalists."

"I don't like only asking them. What presently is foremost in your life?"

"First of all is the festival, which is my big passion now, my baby.
It comes out of the conviction that an artist should be a complete person,

not just aware of art but of how the world works, understanding politics, who owns the world. Being aware. That's why I call it a festival of ideas. It's a platform to present both music and film and in an emotional way and deliver messages. Bring them to this place which is full of truly talented people with exclusive visions, but people who in a strange way are unaware of things, who misunderstand things. I tell you this because when I hear the debate in Poland about world politics by very interesting people, I am always shocked about how little they understand. It's just a repetition of main media messages and major media outlets are not giving you the true image. They give you at best hard truth, but you don't get the inconvenient truth. An artist as a sensitive member of society should not be a naïve participant or victim in the process. The festival is about thinking and becoming a whole person."

"Getting out of the ivory tower…"

"Because it's not a place where we meet to forget the real world. It's a place to deal with reality in a mature way, which is something I admire about you Americans, because even at a funeral, you have this positive energy. The belief that life must go on. We deal with that problem and bury the person with respect, but we also laugh and dance and keep living. And so, the festival is full of joy and full of life, but we also deal with terribly complex issues. That's the philosophy that I wanted to share with you."

Find out more about Jan's festival at http://www.transatlantyk.org.

Gene Gutowski Does Not Need This Interview

It is — or seems to be — a wise sort of thing, to realize that all that happens to a man in this life is only by way of joke, especially his misfortunes, if he has them. And it is also worth bearing in

mind, that the joke is passed round pretty liberally & impartially, so that not very many are entitled to fancy that they in particular are getting the worst of it—Herman Melville, author of Moby Dick

THEY don't make them like Gene Gutowski anymore.

He had it, baby—and whatever it is—he still has it in spades.

That's the bottom line.

Call it style.

Call it elegance.

Call it class, dahling.

The cat is way cool.

I've got personal history with Mr. Gutowski. We first met at a little party in Zoliborz in 1992. I'd been invited to his house because I'd written a profile for The Independent about Gene's production of Ariel Dorfman's Death and the Maiden at Teatr Studio in Warsaw. He liked the piece. I was a roving reporter with fledgling filmmaking ambitions. And there I was in the home of a guru, the man who single-handedly produced Polanski's first three English language films: Repulsion, Cul de Sac, the Fearless Vampire Killers. I knew them well from college film courses. The hostess was a knockout. His fourth wife, Dorota, was 30+ years younger than Gene, a lithe ex-model with sensuous limbs and a magazine-cover face.

Gene was in his mid-sixties then, but in his heart, he was, as always, ageless.

But that was then, and this is now. For the last six weeks, Gene and

I have been dancing. My first email requesting an interview/profile met with a genial and heartfelt, "Nice hearing from you and thanks for asking but not as I no longer give interviews."

Gene was enjoying a winter in St. Martin at a fine hotel on Orient Beach and, well, who could blame him for wanting to be left in peace, already? However, being the ever intrepid reporter, often deaf to the word, "No," I thought I'd give it the old college try once more. We were dancing a slow Mazurka, a kujawiak in 3/4 time. I needed to up the tempo. An oberek was called for.

I've done my share of ass-kissing in show business, so I did what any self-respecting scribbler would do. I waited a week and then wrote the most flattering response I could muster. I got back an elegant (or course!) reply asking if Gene could email me a copy of his book, From Holocaust to Hollywood, which would be easy to read since he wrote it in English. My Polish skills are not what they should be.

Gene continued, "If (the conditional pronoun baby) [it's a conjunction] we do it, could the story centre on the importance of elegance at all times? At 85 I have survived much and occasionally succeeded in life by being elegant." He suggested we do the interview in St. Martin.

"Let me think about it," I wrote back.

Just kidding. I called the boss and told him we were "in." A little Vaseline goes a long way, as Gene would say.

My editor said, "Let me think about it."

Soon the plot hatched. Both Andrzej and I would fly to St Martin. We informed Gene of our plans and booked the trip. Ready to rock and roll. Then on Good Friday, Gene emailed that he had to return to Poland at once. He'd run out of his special heart medicine, and we'd have to do the interview in Warsaw. What the hell, I thought. Who needs an express trip to a Caribbean paradise just on the cusp of spring, right?

Gene returned to Warsaw on a Thursday, and we were to meet the following Monday. Monday morning came and I called. "I'm sorry, my dear. But I just don't feel up to meeting yet. I've got doctors to see, and we are getting ready to move flats…I'm busy on Wednesday with an interview for a French documentary about Roman. "How about Thursday?"

Well, why not? This is the week of the Smolensk catastrophe, so the atmosphere is dolorous and

tense throughout the city, one of those teeth-clenching time warps soaked in weirdness—exactly the opposite of what you want when you are trying to land a Big Fish, and Gene is a Marlin. Make no mistake about that. He knows how to run with the line into the deep water, if you let him. On top of that, Roman Polanski's troubles continue. That's got to hurt. Polanski wrote the epigraphs for Gene's autobiography saying, "Gene is one of the most important characters in my life. Ever since I met him 40 years ago he seems to be present at the most pivotal moments of my existence. I value both his friendship and his professional advice. I'm deeply indebted to him for launching me in my international career, but I do admit that I feel a pang of jealousy that he seems to have managed the first half of his life without me.

(I hadn't seen Gene for several years. I'd been spending a lot of time in the States and in Central America, where one fine day in Nicaragua I ran into a spry 83-year-old New Yorker called Ed Brown Jr., who just happened to be Gene's long lost "cousin" from the early days in New York in the fifties. That was two years ago. I put Ed in touch with Gene and they renewed their acquaintance.)

Now as I rounded the corner into Plac Trzech Krzyzy on a bright April day, I wondered if he still had that certain "je ne sais quoi," that spark, that knowing twinkle in his eye. I wondered how hard a time he was going to give me. I wondered if he was going to offer me a drink. If he did, I knew everything would be okay. I'm used to charming old rogues and their shifty ways. It's like water off a duck's back. That's what I tell myself anyway.

The flat he is leaving is a simple one-bedroom, located in the centre of Warsaw. He lives there surrounded by some prized possessions and objects d'art with his companion of the last decade, the svelte and comely Joanna, a former documentary filmmaker he met while making The Pianist.

The door was standing open as I exited the lift on the fifth floor, and Gene was waiting inside seated on a sofa, Heffner-like in a bathrobe with his nickname "Gucio," embroidered on the back—a gift from one of his sons.

"Just push the door closed," he says.

He welcomes me with that sonorous burr, smooth as a cat's purring and guaranteed to charm. "Hello, how are yaaaa," he drawls—the last word accentuated British-style, but the overall voice relaxed, cool and mid-Atlantic.

"Dr. Gutowski, I presume," I said, feeling like the reporter Stanley finally meeting Livingston in Africa. Warsaw is a jungle after all.

"I brought you a bottle of red," I said.

"You didn't have to do that but thank you very much."

"Least I could do. By the way, I enjoyed your book, Gene."

"Too much sex. Don't you think?"

"Didn't bother me."

"I thought it was too much," he says.

"Why'd you put so much sex in it then?"

"To sell it better. But I overdid it, and that can ruin the effect. On the other hand, I have a wide audience of younger people (smiles). It's a different holocaust story. They couldn't catch me because I was busy fucking somewhere. 'Holofuck' is more like it."

(A throw-away line. You don't hear a lot of Holocaust puns.)

Now we are seated around a large Igor Mitoraj sculptured coffee table. Gene lights a thin cigarette,

sits back and asks with a captive smile, "I see you have your Starbucks coffee. Very American. Now what have you been up to since I last saw you?"

Typical Gene. Always curious about other people. So, I give him a brief rundown and then he

leans forward and sighs, "Now what the fuck do you want from me?"

What indeed? It's hard to be finite on an infinite subject, especially when the subject is an expert storyteller who has done things that most men would give their left nut to have, if not done, at least witnessed. For example, do you want to talk about women that Malemen would love? The mind reels. He produced the film that made Catherine Deneuve an international star (Repulsion). He gave Jacqueline Bisset her first screen test (Cul de Sac). He was once pictured in the French tabloids with Brigitte Bardot at the door to her Paris flat (he was subbing for Warren Beatty who'd instinctively ducked around the corner to avoid paparazzi hiding in the bushes). He produced the film during which the most star-crossed of famous couples, Sharon Tate and Roman Polanski, became lovers (The Fearless Vampire Killers). He was a habitué of The Playboy Club Casino in London in the late sixties when that was the most hell-raising club in the world with regular guests including the Beatles and the Stones and an A-list of film celebrities from both sides of the Atlantic.

Take a breath.

"Let's start with the importance of being elegant, why not?"

Gene lifts his glass, "just a little beer," to wet his whistle.

"Look," he starts in slowly and deliberately, "I came from an elegant family and grew up used to the finer things of life. Eugene was not my real name. It was Witold, which I had to change during the War…"

Gene! Perfect! His assumed name, Eugene, means "well born," and suggests something inherited,

something in the genes, as it were. He was born Witold Bardach into a secular Jewish family—his immediate family vanished in the Holocaust—and into a Poland that no longer exists. The town, Rawa Ruska near Lvov, became part of Ukraine in 1945.

"So, I'm coming out of Europe the sole survivor of a famous family. Everybody got killed off. You lose family but you don't lose your sense of entitlement. You come to accept certain standards of conduct…"

Loss. A week of loss. A life of loss. An old Polish story. Gene retreats from the sitting room to his office and returns slowly—he walks, but not so well anymore—clutching a heavy album full of photos. A telling fact: In his memoirs the first twenty-two years of his life take up half the book, which ends with the making of The Pianist. His sharp focus on his youth (especially considering its circumstances) is not unusual amongst men who have done great things, witnessed great events.

"I can show you photographs that I came from very elegant, cultured people. Even living in a small town near Lvov my mother read a French newspaper every day. My father spoke five languages and because of his linguistic abilities he was a liaison to English and French officers during the Bolshevik War."

Indeed, it was Gene's knowledge of languages, including fluent German and English, which saved him during the war, not to mention a certain savoir faire, which included always being well-groomed and well-dressed.

Gene's always had a genius for survival and re-inventing himself.

"Who was going to kill an elegant young man who spoke fluent German? Are you crazy?" he says. Now he points out his beloved uncle Andrew who, like his father, was a role model, "a very sophisticated man," who was shipped out to a Gulag from Lvov. Later he joined Anders' army in Persia and was in all the campaigns in Africa and Italy.

Gene says, "Now he was an elegant man, and his wife came from an elegant family and after the war they immigrated to Brazil. Of course, I thought he was dead too. Then after the war I was talking to someone in New York and mentioned I'd lost my uncle Andrew in the war. He said, 'what are you talking about? You didn't lose him. I just saw him boarding a ship for Brazil.' He'd been employed as the head of a Firestone factory for some years in Sao Paulo."

Gene brought Uncle Andrew over to London in the eighties and bought him an apartment right next to his. "It gave him another five years of good life. He died in 1990. He was then 87. He was a very, very cultured, sophisticated man."

The caption under Uncle Andrew's photographs from the 1930s reads, "Always Elegant and Handsome."

Is there a specific instance where being elegant saved his neck?

Gene says: "Well, even before I needed my neck saved, when I was 15 or 16, I fancied myself as a great lover and a great seducer. I remember using three different colognes, including one for my hands to touch their lovely faces. You know, I was crazy."

He points to another picture and says, "My uncle Bronislaw, the dentist, was insanely elegant. He had his suits made in England. Remember there was no ready-to-wear back then. He drove a large Packard with two windshields and enormous headlights. I don't know where he even got that from."

And then softly he adds, "He was a bit of a prick actually."

"All right, now here's a photo of my uncle. Look at him! Bronislaw's wife drove a Bugatti, and he drove that Packard…Here, he is wearing patent leather shoes with his uniform. I mean who does that? Crazy! Still, it shows you a bit of style in a regimental photo from the 1921 war."

So, his background was the key to his survival?

"Absolutely," Gene says without a shadow of a doubt. "I call it a sense of entitlement. That is who I am and this is what I respect. Let's face it. I had a problem. My entire family was killed off in 1942…for being Jewish. They just couldn't save themselves. Sometimes I've held it against my poor father that he thought of trying to save his parents before saving himself and his children. Anyway, I came to Warsaw but with the knowledge that I had to be elegant within the means I had.

Sometimes I was hungry. I don't remember a single time during the whole occupation that I didn't shave because once you stop shaving, I thought, you let yourself go. And razor blades were not easy to get. You used to sharpen them inside a glass."

Elegance of mind and good tailoring were survival tools. Grace, good humour and youthful daring were an invisible cloak worn against the slings and arrows of outrageous fortune. Good form was a way to beat the devil at this own game. But was he courageous?

"Courageous? I don't know. I was totally foolish. I'm not a physically courageous man. I'm not the type to jump into a river to save someone. I want to say also that people have different standards. They do different things under pressure… informing or collaborating with the Germans. None of that for me… Sometimes you hide under the lantern. Sometimes it's best to hide where there's the most light."

Famously, he smuggled Luftwaffe radios to the AK while working in the Junker factory in Warsaw. Was that the scariest time of his life?

Gene pauses and chuckles. He lights another thin cigarette. "The scariest moment? Believe it or not an American officer scared the shit out of me. It was Germany after the war. I was stationed in Starnberg, and I was courting this American lady, Zillah Rhoads from Culpeper, Virginia. We used to travel all over the place sightseeing on the weekend. Being in the CIC (US Counterintelligence Corps) I could go where I wished. So, we went to visit some of those palaces near Munich built by that crazy King Ludwig. We were on a boat on the lake. I always had to carry a pistol, which this time I'd put in my briefcase. When I had to pay for the trip I opened the briefcase, and the German conductor of that little boat saw the pistol. So, he got immediately got on the phone and called the American Military police saying, "You'd better get over here, there's a man with a gun." So, at that point we are getting into my elegant convertible slowly, slowly and suddenly a jeep rolls up with a young lieutenant MP who approaches, obviously scared shitless. He has a big .45 pointed right at my nose and his hand is shaking. Well, you don't want to be hit by a .45. I put my hands up. He says, "Where's your gun?" and I explained carefully who I was and why I could carry the gun. And that was my scariest moment of the war because he had a cocked and loaded gun pointed at me."

So, you were almost killed by the people you were working for? Is that a metaphor for life?

"Well, you never know," says Gene. "The MP was young and nervous, and he could have gotten off by saying he had to kill me in the line of duty and so forth."

The moral of that story is the key to success in life.

"Don't be afraid… Or, at least, don't show it," says Gene. "Make the most of your situation whatever it is and do it with class. For example, there we were at the end of the war when Germany was destroyed and poor. Zillah and I wanted to arrange our wedding at St Lukas cathedral in Munich. It was an evening wedding and I had to organize the whole thing. Black market coal to heat the church. A wedding cake from the army PX in Garmisch—a beautiful three-tier cake. I drove from Garmisch in a jeep with one hand on the wheel and one on the cake. I needed formal wear for the evening event but had no tails, so I borrowed them from a rather portly doctor I knew in Garmisch. Unfortunately, I had to have them taken in. Poor fellow. I never told him what happened, so when he got them back, he must've thought he'd put on a lot of weight. Always elegant and handsome.

Familiarity with danger may make a brave man braver, but it usually makes them less daring. Not so, in Gene's case, though he would deny it if I said it to his face.

Here's a case in point. We've all heard of clothes to die for. It's a saying. But what about clothes to kill for? We are not talking about browsing through the duty-free at Schiphol or shopping for Armani in Milan.

"Do you know how I got my first suit after the war? Through thick and thin throughout the war I had kept this suit that I had tailored in Warsaw. That was so that at the end of the war I'd put on the suit and be elegant."

Of course. You'd do the same wouldn't you, dear reader?

So, imagine. It's Spring 1945. Everyone's dashing through Austria to the German border chased by the Russians. All Gene has is his tattered Organization Todt [???] uniform. He'd been forced into working for the Nazi civil and military engineering corps. After days of walking amidst refugees of all stripes, he'd stowed his rucksack on a wagon, so he didn't have to carry it. Then here come the Russian tanks to cut off the group before they made it to the American sector.

Gene legs it fast as he can.

"I was in pretty good shape then, 19 years old—not like now."

He makes it to the bridge, crosses over the Ems River into the hands of the Americans. But he'd left the suit on the wagon! That wouldn't do. His Todt uniform would make him a marked man. The Americans were still trying to gather up uniformed people and put them in POW camps. Gene had to ditch the uniform and get some proper clothes in a hurry.

What to do in such a sartorial crisis?

The Gutowski solution: "I wandered into this little town nearby and kept looking till I saw a sign for a tailor, Schneider. I went in and basically committed armed robbery to get the poor guy to provide a suit.

Fortunately, he had some suits on the rack that hadn't been collected. I selected a dark blue one. He made a few alterations and once he realized I wasn't going to shoot him, his wife brought out some tea and cakes which we proceeded to enjoy while I browsed around and picked out some shirts, a tie and some shoes."

Talk about cornering the market in chutzpah. His language skills and his suit, according to Gene, impressed American officers so much that pretty soon he was interrogating Germans for the US Counter-Intelligence Corps and having his suits made in Munich.

"You know, I found a glove-maker in Munich and eventually had 19 pairs of gloves made. That was me," he says with a shrug as he points to a photo of himself in uniform in Paris. He is standing on a virtually deserted Champs Elysees of an afternoon wearing a glove on his left hand and clutching the other in his right.

Gene says, "You either have style or you don't. What can I tell you?

"So, whether you have a million bucks or not, you say 'this is me and I'm somebody.' Is that it?" I ask.

"The important thing is to look like a million bucks," says Gene. "Alright, that's enough for today. I'm a little tired."

He's right. It wouldn't be polite to intrude any longer. Besides he's eighty-fucking-five. This is a magazine story, not an assassination attempt. That said...I still didn't get my drink.

* * *

AFTER another necessary postponement—this is Gene Gutowski after all—we finally meet again a few days later. Gene and Joanna are packing. The Smolensk funerals are over. The atmosphere is brighter. Gene seems more rested. The jetlag has faded. Things are looking up. I have brought another bottle of wine and twenty yellow tulips for Joanna.

After we are seated on separate sofas around the Mitoraj table, Gene says, "Would you like a drink?"

"Absolutely," I say.

"How about a little whisky?"

Joanna produces some Johnnie Walker Black and kindly pours us a couple of splashes.

"No rocks," she says.

So, Gene and I sip it neat.

I start off by asking Gene advice about whether or not I should buy a nice Italian suit I've spotted, exactly my size, 42L, in a second-hand shop in my neighbourhood. The only problem is that it's kind of well... brown leaning to rust colour. I usually favour solid black or dark grey pinstripe. "You can carry that off. With my colouring I couldn't," says Gene. "Most of the really good clothes I ever bought were bought in London, but that's been a while. Style has changed, perhaps even disintegrated, the elegant and the chic blended with kitsch. Casual style is more a personal revelation than a coded uniform suggesting status. Billionaires dress down, but princes still dress up.

Gene jumps on the subject. "Generally, my generation dressed to look older like our fathers," says Gene. "Now old men try to dress like their kids. In the fifties, whatever elegance there was in the US, it was on the eastern seaboard with Brooks Brothers (which Gene favours nowadays). Tripler and Paul Stuart lead the way with Dunhill for Blazers, Lock for hats, which we all wore, and Lobb for shoes, though I always preferred the light Italian Testoni of which I've had a fine pair for over 30 years. England was of course a paradise for men's clothing since the days of the Regency dandies and London is still a Mecca for all the things a well-appointed man could wish for from Saville Row tailors to shirt makers on Jermyn Street like Harvey Hudson or Turnbull and Asser with Daks for trousers and Holland and Holland for the hunting and sporting man. There are countless places for canes, umbrellas, colognes, hairdressing etc. etc. Until recently there were few places for ladies to shop... On the whole, we, Americans (Gene is a citizen of both the US and Poland) have problems with elegance mostly because of our bulk. As they say, you can never be too rich or too thin. I remember in my days in the Virgin Islands in the 80s, a suave Italian called Flavio Briatore, later the owner of a Formula One team, tried to open and run a branch of Regine's night club and failed miserably. While the locals, many of them black of course, would dress up splendidly with good trousers and a shirt, the Americans seemed to insist that it was their birth right to show up at night in sweaty t-shirts exposing hairy backs with dirty shorts and sandals. In Florida old men run around in shorts and Nike shoes, and California? Forget it. Only the British upper class had the right attitude to being casually elegant. I remember once being invited to a formal pheasant shoot. I had to wear a tie and beat the hell out of my tweed suit for it to look properly old and worn out... Italy of course had great tailors with Caracene and Schifonelli and Angelo's all together leading the way on the Via Condotti in Rome. Gucci too. Today there is obviously Armani and Zegna but for mass consumption… It's a pity that Polish society doesn't have this elegance of spirit which translates into the other stuff anymore. Because by acts of omission and commission the whole middle class was eliminated, the landed gentry gone, the Jews gone. This whole society now has peasant roots. They come from small villages and towns…In 1940 there were 80,000 people with higher education in Poland and they killed 22,000 of them in Katyn!"

Doesn't this lack of grace, if you will, translate to contemporary culture as a whole, including films? "Listen I don't give a fuck about contemporary culture," Gene says with a pleasant laugh.

Gene was always a big picture guy. No pun intended.

"You asked me a question. Here's the short answer. My father said it takes 24 years not eight to make a gentleman. Three generations of gymnasium. Who taught people how to dress and how to eat during the war and under communism? Still, Poland has made a giant step forward in the last twenty years. You could even see it in connection with the recent catastrophe. I was amazed at the number of men in dark well-cut suits. The Prime Minister is obviously a Zegna man."

Gene's priorities bring to mind something Miles Davis once said, "For me music and life is all about style."

For Gene, the swinging sixties in London were his finest hour. Filmmaking and life were all about style—maybe even style as fetish.

"I like the British and did well in London. What a time! Plenty of style. Doug Heyward was the tailor to celebs. He started very small working with a Ukrainian called Dimitri, who had a tailoring outfit in Fulham. Doug was the front man who came to your house and did the measurements. He opened a place in Mount Street later. I remember when Roman came to London in '63 and tore up his only pair of trousers. Dougie did the repairs for him. You go into his shop and gossip and meet friends. Everyone had suits made by Heyward. I even had a suit made for Uncle Andrew and his suits were very special because they required 20 pockets. He carried absolutely everything with him that he thought he might need."

Gene might be termed one of the Princes of London during the swinging sixties. He was as hip as you could get. He went to London to make a Sherlock Holmes series for TV and ended up staying. The series didn't come off, yet he made a fun but forgettable film called Station Six Sahara starring Carol Baker (a siren of the time) and so found a start in the movie business. It was a tight little group. Everybody knew everybody. In March 1963, when he married his second wife, Judy, a model, the entire film industry was at the wedding in the registry office and then everyone went to his house in Montpelier Street.

Impossible as it is to believe now, London was a cheap place to live. And making movies was easier.

"Here's the thing," says Gene. "Back then you were the producer. One producer. Now you watch the print of Repulsion, Cul de Sac or the Vampire Killers and there's one producer. Gene Gutowski. Now you see a picture. The producer credits go on and on. The agent wants a producer credit. The guy who makes sandwiches wants a credit too. In those days there was one producer. That's it. It was a lovely cosy business then in England. All the major Hollywood studios had their offices in London, and these guys were easily accessible."

You had more responsibility, but more control. You got the rewards and the blame.

"Exactly," says Gene. "But making pictures was much, much cheaper, too."

"In today's climate a film like Repulsion (1965) probably wouldn't get made. Were you aware how special this film was while you were making it?"

Gene is laughing now.

"No. Oh, my god, no! We were just taking a picture. We thought it was great but when it came out and Bosley Crowther, who was a big critic at the New York Times, said he thought it was something everyone should see, we knew we were home free."

I wonder if he has been running from or toward something all his life. We all might ask ourselves the same question.

"Just running," says Gene.

Just running.

Through the war. Through the American intelligence service. Through New York in the 1950s. Through London in the sixties. Through films that worked and films that didn't Through businesses of many stripes. Sic transit Gloria mundi…Through four marriages out of which he salvaged his most prized achievement, his three sons and their grandchildren.

Family is still constantly on his mind.

"I started life in total denial," Gene says. "I invented a completely new identity. I beat up on myself. I never admitted I was Jewish. Not even to my own family. Not until a few years ago. It wasn't about being

Jewish. To start with I have absolutely no religious training. In our home they used to slaughter pigs for Easter and make sausages. Not very Jewish, is it?"

We're looking through old photographs again now.

There he is, smiling with his friends by a swimming pool, circa 1943, in the depths of war when in his spare time he's stealing radios from the Germans. How is one able to do that?

"You don't show fear," he says slowly. "The trouble with the Jews was that even when they had the so-called "right look," it was the fear in their eyes that gave them away. I never had fear in my eyes." And he still doesn't, just that same sparkle that resonates from the old black and white photo.

What are the other things that are most important in life?

"Having enough money to enjoy yourself, and friends who are loyal."

What was the worst mistake he ever made?

"Turning down Stanley Kubrick and Mike Nichols. I was too ambitious. I'd been promised a three-picture deal. So, I blew off Mike Nichols and Kubrick. Bye bye! Poor Mike Nichols even borrowed Burton's apartment at the Dorchester to impress me, a schmuck from Lvov. It's too painful to discuss. It's definitely the biggest mistake I ever made business-wise."

"You can't really make a bigger business mistake than firing Kubrick and Nichols."

"It's difficult to beat," I say.

His greatest experience?

"The Pianist was a good one. I suppose you could call that payback for all the denials."

In your autobiography you wrote about trying to analyse the effect of the loss of your family on your pursuit of the good life over the perspective of time, about realizing loss and the pain that goes with it. I can only wonder what it must be like.

Gene pauses and says slowly, "I'm like so many people who came out of the Holocaust who are unable to deal with the tragedy and the losses. You want to go into complete denial, put out of your mind what happened to you, invent a new curriculum vitae for yourself...put out of your mind what you've experienced, what you've seen. How else can you deal as a 15, 16-year-old boy when practically overnight the entire family is wiped out? Your grandparents, your cousins, your uncles, everybody. You're alone. You're a fucking orphan. The worst part of it is I had a young brother who was left behind in Lvov and who wrote me a desperate letter once to help him and I wasn't able to. That's excusable. How could I have helped him? Yet the sense of guilt has been with me throughout my life. I should've been my brother's keeper. I couldn't have been. You know? These are the issues, and you submerge yourself in life, in women in sexuality. I've done it all. You name it...You live with a tremendous sense of loss, which as I get older is getting stronger and stronger, but I was fortunate that I was able to extend my life because I have three sons, and they have children, so I see the continuation of the family, which otherwise would've been wiped out. In the end life wins over death. Right? That's the essence of it. You see this may sound vain and is because in a way I probably am a vain man, but I am very proud of the genetic background. I have a very handsome family on both sides, and I see the continuation of the good genes in my children and their children and that makes me very happy. They are good-looking, intelligent, creative and successful at what they do. Life wins.

Continuing...

"For example, nothing pleased me more than a vast collection of beautiful London tailored suits that

I was able to give to my son Andrew, who is exactly the same size as I was way back when. With that gift he became the best dressed real estate developer and architect in America. My other son, Adam, is a documentary film producer who has a film about Halston (the iconic seventies designer) in the Tribeca Film Festival this month. My other son has been a yacht captain based in Monte Carlo for years."

Gene smiles.

Bon mots from a bon vivant.

"In this way even, elegance carries on. I've assured myself of the continuation of life afterwards..."

Andrei Konchalovsky: Twice in a Lifetime

He is his own work of art. Russia meets America. Tango and Cash meets Andrei Rublev. He wrote and directed Stallone and wrote with Tarkovsky—which must qualify as the height of Darwinian adaptability. He survived the Soviet triumph and opprobrium to suffer and succeed in Hollywood. His films have won at Cannes and been nominated for Oscars. And he recently directed what may be the biggest box office flop of all time. It cost $90 million, made $300,000. How does he do it? "There's no substitute for luck," he says. He is not a mere survivor, now in his seventies he's still a pioneer.

His latest film, Nutcracker 3D, which is part of the retrospective being presented at the Sputnik Film Festival in Warsaw, was strangled at birth by US critics, who couldn't handle his brutal treatment of the perennially saccharine subject. Nutcracker has a 0% rating on Rotten Tomatoes, the film-rating website. The Americans hated it.

Konchalovsky says: "I think it was the most expensive independent movie of all time. I wanted to make a film that was very original, but it's hard for such a film to be successful in the American market. It was a failure because there was no major promotion attached and I found myself on an island with a film that no one wants to see. Now it's coming out slowly, but it is having a hard time because the American market killed the movie. The reviews were horrible. Terrible! How did Konchalovsky come up with this idea? Why are their rats in German uniforms? What bullshit!"

His brother's recent film, Burnt by the Sun 2 hasn't fared much better. The Russians hated Nonetheless... In the West, Konchalovsky (AK) is best known for Hollywood movies, such as action-epic Runaway Train (Jon Voight, Eric Roberts), Tango and Cash (Sylvester Stallone, Kurt Russell) and the excellent Shy People, a film set deep in the Louisiana bayous for which the usually luscious Barbara Hershey won Best Actress at the 1987 Cannes Film Festival as a cantankerous Cajun survivor. His Uncle Vanya (1970) may be the best adaptation of Chekhov ever.

* * *

Artists don't come with better pedigrees than Andrei Konchalovsky. He is the offspring of a clan rooted in Russian culture. The Mikhalkovs were part of the elite in the tsarist and Stalin eras. They still are today.

Rewind. His great-grandfather on his mother's side was Russian painter Vasily Surikov, who was inexplicably a Bolshevik favourite. (Who knew?) His great grandfather was an imperial governor of the city of Yaroslavl. His father, Sergei, who died last summer aged 96, wrote the lyrics to both the Soviet and the Russian Federation's national anthems. His uncle, Mikhail, was a war hero who wrote a book about his exploits as a spy. His brother, the director, Nikita Mikhailov, has won both the Grand Prix at Cannes and an Oscar (Burnt by the Sun, 1994). Konchalovsky took his moniker from his grandfather on his mother's side, the artist, Pyotr Konchalovsky. Are you ready for this? He is even distantly related to Mr. T. Not B. A. Baracus (A-Team) but the biggest T of them all: Tolstoy.

About his famous brother: Well, there are differences besides being different psychological types. I am quite cerebral, and I like doubts. I'm much more a European than my brother. He is an emotional man, poetic, very religious. So, in many things we are completely different, and at the same time, there is the difference of birth. I am the older brother. It means that for the first part of my life I was the leader. He was the follower. But then as time passes the younger brother finds his own path and that's when he starts to compete. I compete with Bertolucci. I don't compete with Nikita. About his choice of Konchalovsky over Mikhailov as his name: At first, I simply used a pseudonym. I think decided to use the name of my mother and my grandfather because my father and I were so different. It wasn't so much a matter of dissension as just having a different perspectives. My father was a product of the pre-war period. He was a writer during the Great Purges (1930s). I began writing when there was a revolution, which I was very happy about, in Hungary in 1956.

* * *

It's a Friday in mid-October. AK's talking to me via Skype video from his office in Moscow.

WRR: Andrei? Can you hear me?... I can see you... Andrei?

AK: Yes, I can hear you now.

WRR: So, how's it going today?

AK: Same as always... In the middle somewhere... Not too bad... I think the most important thing is not to feel worse.

WRR: I'm sorry I wasn't able to get to Moscow to meet you in person, but I look [???]

AK: Yes, it's a pity.

WRR: I understand that Russians consider it good manners to ask about the current situation in the country. So how are things in the Federation?

AK: Neither here nor there... We are in the waiting room. People are waiting for some leader, person who is going to make things a lot better for them... without having to do it for themselves. They don't want to do things themselves rather they want someone in power to tell them what to do. Russians like a father figure. It's in our history.

WRR: You have mentioned before a resurgent feudalism or medievalism in contemporary Russia. Is that the foreseeable future?

AK: Oh yes. These things cannot change in the span of one life. It takes a long time. But I think the main reason we have this medieval attitude is that we never had a bourgeoisie as a class. It's through the middle class that you get a society of citizens and a class that is independent from the ruling class. It's as basic as that.

WRR: What role does Russian mysticism play in this?

AK: I think that Eastern Orthodox religion didn't give Russians a basis in western philosophy based on Roman ideas. Instead, we got the Slavic point of view without the range of western wisdom because... Europe is based on the values of Jerusalem, Athens and Rome. Christianity was based on these philosophical points of wisdom. And the Orthodox mind simply doesn't follow the same rules. That's why Russians look to the East more than to the West. It's a very complicated matter because if you look at the history of Eastern European civilization there was a moment of bifurcation when Russian power chose an eastern alliance. And in one sense Russia was invaded by Tartars and Mongols and it was a logical thing after that to choose an eastern alliance, for example much easier than with the Poles. I remain absolutely convinced that the Iron Curtain was not so much a result of a clash between socialism or communism and capitalism or democratic society but because of these ancient philosophical differences.

WRR: I've always thought that the United States and Russia were two sides of the same coin. Recently a colleague of mine rode his motorbike across Russia to Mongolia and back and he is of the same opinion. Do you see any similarities?

AK: I think that they are so different that they have ended up similar. I say this because Russians believe in Fate. Russian mentality values luck. Russians think that suffering is the path to improvement. All this was well laid out by Dostoyevsky. American society is based on middle class individualism. The Russian mentality is based on feudalism. And now the intolerance of fundamentalist Americans, a kind of jihad, is maybe even closer to fascism. Then there is the dictatorship of political correctness, controlling thought... And don't forget there's another basic difference. Americans say that time is money. There is no concept of this in Russia. For us time and money are two different things. And remember: America is a country of laws. By comparison Russia is lawless.

Konchalovsky has written recently of Russia as a Mobster Land, a society with no real citizens, dominated by peasant consciousness with loyalties limited to the family and where everything outside the family circle is regarded as hostile.

WRR: So how are the US and Russia the same?

AK: Well, they both came to power but by opposite routes. American society is based on the dictatorship of law. Russia is based on lack of law. There is no law in Russia. I mean there are, but no one follows them. Russia is much closer to Mexico.

WRR: Maybe you are waiting for Pancho Villa...

AK: Maybe. (laughs) Americans have done everything possible to change Mexico but it hasn't worked.

* * *

WRR: How hard was it to make the transition from the USSR to America in the 1980s?

AK: It was very difficult, but I had some right to leave because I had a French wife. The transition was easy in practical terms but emotionally it was very difficult. It was hard to get into regular American life for me. The transition was not very easy to understand, coming from a society which didn't allow direct criticism to a completely free situation where everything goes. And in America, I had to learn to sell myself, my talent. In Russia, I was a graduate of film school, which gave me the right to direct films, so I just had to wait in line to make a film. I was expected to make films, you see. You just couldn't openly criticize Soviet Russia. That's it. In the United States I had to sell myself, my ideas. If you can't do that, then you're in the shit. I had to learn this over several years. I couldn't understand why people weren't running to me to ask me to make a film."

(laughter)

WRR: You could have said, "Hey, I made Siberiade (1979). That's a great one! Haven't you seen it? It's four and a half hours long. It's longer than Gone with the Wind. It won the Jury Prize at Cannes!" So how did you make the transition... to selling your ideas?

Andrei reaches to his left to get his coffee.

WRR: I should have mentioned your coffee since I can see it and you can't. Anyway, I can have mine at the same time and we can share the same sensory experience.

AK: You know it's a very strange society we're living in now. I think pretty soon people are going to be having sex on Skype.

WRR: They already do, I'm sure.

AK: We are kind of mental masturbators.

WRR: That's the point of an interview. To give people something to read when they are in the bathroom.

AK: Here's an interesting thing. You know when I went to a party in Hollywood—by Hollywood I mean the big studios not the independent filmmakers—I often found myself in the bathroom reading a magazine because the party was so boring. But I missed the point. Because the most important thing is not talent. It is connections. And I never had connections there. That's why I failed at first.

WRR: The cocaine connection was the one you needed to make. That's what you should have been doing in the bathroom, Andrei, instead of reading.

AK: Perhaps, but I don't like losing control of myself. That's why I prefer booze.

WRR: What's your booze of choice.

AK: Tequila

WRR: Which kind?

AK: Same as with vodka. In Russia we have a saying. There are only two kinds of vodka: good and better... But I like tequila because it creates the desire to make revolution.

WRR: So, did tequila help you to make a revolution within yourself in order to get on in Hollywood?

AK: (laughter) I did adapt. But here's the thing: When I arrived, there was still a place for a message and for veracity in films. You could still make films like China Syndrome. There was space for individual vision. But when Wall Street came to Hollywood, it came under the control of lawyers and bankers. And of course, there was the extraordinary explosion of the Star Wars-type films. When I saw Star Wars the first time, I thought it's nice but it's a stupid story. It was a fairy-tale made with special effects. Very stylized. Anyway, that was the moment Hollywood began to be the focus of the bankers and they began to take over. Hollywood became focused on pure entertainment. Then of course sport became even bigger than movies. And the biggest stars were football, baseball and basketball stars. Films were being made for people who don't like to read. Previously they made films based on classic books like for example, The Great Gatsby. Hollywood had been making films from class American prose. And that's finished. I'm talking about Hollywood, not the independents. The American film industry is not only Hollywood. American film art is found in the independents. If you look at the way new films are distributed, you see the difference.

WRR: So, what was the good part about working in Hollywood?

AK: Shooting. For me it's always a personal adventure. It's like being a skydiver. It's like that. It's a breath-taking experience as if you are chasing the dream… I think the worst moment for a filmmaker is when people laugh when you want them to cry, and they are sad when you want them to laugh. Some director said—I can't remember who— that when you start to shoot a film you think you are a genius and by the time you finish you are thinking what the hell can I do to save this piece of shit?

WRR: How did you learn to play the Hollywood game?

AK: Hunger.

WRR: That will do it.

AK: Sure, but first I got a job teaching in a film school. Then I didn't want to be in the club of "losers."

WRR: Being a teacher?

AK: No, being a director who can't make films because no one wants him. But I wasn't alone. There were a number of wonderful American directors who couldn't get money to make a film.

WRR: Hackman and Al Pacino. 1973. Great film.

AK: Yeah. So, the "club" was full of directors who can't find money for their ideas… so then I had luck because Jon Voigt saw Siberiade, and he picked me up and invited me to write a script… If you want to be successful in Hollywood, you have to be willing to work as a waiter. Nowadays you have to be willing to shoot a film for 1000 dollars and show it and be noticed. It's possible to do that. To make a twenty-minute film and show it at Sundance and get noticed. You know there is a Hollywood saying: There's no failure. Only comebacks. The real mark of the artist is to stay true to yourself and come back.

The Man in the White Suit, The Stig

Tor Poznan. The racetrack. A windy Friday in late February. 12.30 p.m. The Stig said, "Get in." It was an offer I couldn't refuse. And yet... and yet... I was hitching a ride with a driver who is notorious for knowing two things about ducks. And they are both wrong. Trackside, the TVN Turbo people were throwing fits, horrified, pointing at their watches. "No, No! There's no time!"

Ben repeated, "Just get in. We'll take a short spin." He wanted to show me the curve, the one that almost "finished me," as he put it. (Perhaps I should have thought twice before I jumped in with him.)

"Put your seat belt on in case I kill you," he says. At high speeds there is always the possibility that something will go horribly wrong. That's where the thrill is. Ha ha ha ha ha! Eat my dust Turbo Freaks! We're hauling ass!

The Infiniti lurched forward picking up speed and soon we were drifting, almost floating, through the first curve, Ben over steering, causing a loss of traction in the rear wheels, the front wheels pointing in the opposite direction of the turn, yet smoothly controlled from the entry to exit of the corner. Your stomach jumps. Adrenalin pumps. A few days before I had been motorcycling through the impossibly crowded streets of Margoa in India floating in streams of sunshine and insane traffic and now Vroooooooom, we hit the straight track and into another drift and a straight and a drift and into the straight and OFF THE TRACK and just as quickly back on again.

"Just a touch of rallying for you," Ben said.

"I know what kind of person you are now," the TVN PR woman, Marta, said as we roared back to a screeching halt. I was grinning like Jack Nicholson in The Shining. I would have howled at the moon if it had been midnight instead of midday.

Because speed is the ultimate adrenalin high.

His job with TVN Turbo is to drive test cars "to destruction," says the former Stig, Ben Collins. "I'm pushing really, really hard. These are all road cars, and they can't do more than two or three laps before the brakes start to go. What we are trying to do, perhaps unlike Top Gear, is to really see the weaknesses and the strengths of the cars, to find their limits. There's no bullshit in this." The Stig, if you happened not to know, is the masked test driver from the BBC car show Top Gear, which has 350 million viewers worldwide, making the Stig the most famous unknown celebrity on the planet. There have been three Stigs: Perry McCarthy (2002-2003), Ben Collins (2003-2010) and Unknown (2010-2012). For seven years Ben Collins was an anonymous legend, a masked man who, despite his racing prowess, was taunted relentlessly by show host Jeremy Clarkson, who maintained that the Stig was kept mute and incognito because racing drivers are stupid, and their opinions are worthless. In the very first show, Clarkson said, "We don't know its name, we really don't know its name, nobody knows its name, and we don't want to know because it's a racing driver."

In his "Some say" introductions, Clarkson claimed variously that the Stig was confused by stairs and afraid of bells, that he had hydraulic legs and two sets of knees, that he never blinked and naturally faced magnetic north, that he could catch fish with his tongue and that he invented the curtain, that his left nipple made the shape of Nürburgring racetrack, and that the BBC paid his salary in pornography. For his trip to the Isle of Man Road Test, the Stig was picked up like cargo from the baggage conveyor at the airport. That was the shtick. Great stuff! One hoax in 2008 revealed the Stig to be Michael Schumacher.

Of such stuff pop legend is quite rightly born. If the Stig had been a rock band, he would have been Kiss. If he had been a caped crusader, he would have been Batman (who also liked to drive fast). If he had been a spy, he would have been Bond. (Collins' company did the stunt driving for the last two Bond films.) If he were an artist, he would be Banksy, who hid his identity for years until outed by The Daily Mail.

But what is a Stig? Clarkson coined the term based on his English public-school days at Repton where "Stig" was a nickname for new boys from "Stigma" which in English means "a mark of disgrace associated with a particular circumstance, quality, or person." (Worth noting: Stig is a Swedish first name and a region in Serbia.)

It all ended in tears in 2010 with a lawsuit. Collins went public with his autobiography and the BBC sued his publisher. Clarkson whined, "If you have seen Wall Street, Greed is not good, kids. It was a shock. I had him over for drinks at the house and all the time he was writing a book.

Collins maintains that the BBC had already outed him: "What happened was that the (BBC) Radio Times did a story headlined: Who is the Stig? The Nation Wants to Know. They did aphoto shoot with a guy dressed in the white suit and inside is a photo of me and another candidate who is in his late 50s. That happened in 2008 and the first I knew about it was when our plumber came in with a copy of the magazine and asked me to sign it. He said we all know you are the Stig so can you please sign it? Within three months of that happening it ran in all the national papers. So, I knew they were planning to get rid of me."

The courts decided in favour of the Stig. He moves in mysterious ways. The Top Gear gang responded by doing a drive-by shooting of cardboard Stig cut-outs. Boys will be boys.

* * *

I have noticed on occasion that the right dose of Xanax and red wine will produce a jovial mood, however accompanied by the side effect of weirdly slurred speech. My voice seems to morph into an oddly mellifluous mixture of Marlon Brando's mumbling in The Godfather and Dean Martin's crooning of My Rifle, My Pony and Me with a dash of lisping Churchill. It was with this voice that I approached His Holiness, the Stig, who most people just call Ben these days.

"So, who are you?" he asks me.

"I'm the Stig of reporters so I can't reveal my identity. But truthfully, if I tell you who I am, I don't have to kill you. I have to kill myself."

Ben laughs.

"But seriously, can you tell me the two things you don't know about ducks?"

"I can't remember them," he says. Despite what Clarkson says, Collins is a sharp cookie. He did a law degree and then spent four years in the army.

How did he learn to drive?

"On my 18th birthday my dad gave me the present of a try-out. I always wanted to be a fighter pilot and when I got in the car, I thought I was Tom Cruise in Top Gun… There was something about getting in the car. I already felt that was the place to be before I drove it. It was a kind of an emotional connection and I drove flat out and nearly set a record my first time (at Silverstone racing school). Then I went to America to do Indy Light cars. I had a great year racing, but I didn't make the cut and came home with my tail between my legs. I kept on until I was 26 and the racing team ended. Then I was in the army reserve and started teaching evasive driving, which is great fun. The interesting thing is that you learn all these dirty tricks in racing. They teach them to you. Most kids start racing go carts when they are six or seven years old, post embryo stage. They already had this ability to tap your car in the right place to slip past, so you learn that very quickly—not just car control of your own car but of theirs as well, so how to nudge or push their car like they do in NASCAR."

"What separates the sheep from the goats in racing?"

"Hard to say really. I'm built the way I am. I love the high speeds. You have that or you don't. I love the high-speed corners. That mentality suits Le Mans. For example, they have a corner there called Indianapolis because it's the fastest corner in the world. At 185 miles an hour you just lift off the gas and turn right and it's really exciting. But you see the consequences, if anything goes wrong… a big fireball and it's really unpleasant sometimes… There was a qualifying run one time and I saw a guy crash and there was his head in his helmet lying beside the track."

How does that affect you?

"You never think it will happen to you… Le Mans is a huge race. The track is 81/2 miles long so it's twice as long as any other. The first time you go there it's a big thing because the speeds are like at Indy. 250 miles an hour. It's for the big boys. You have to have something in you to want to be there in the first place. Does that make sense? And the other thing is that Le Mans is really a long race (24 hrs), so you get all kinds of weather. In my first year it rained for 17 hours, and we were quickest in the rain. I caught up two laps. We got up to fourth place and were catching the leaders when the car broke down."

What qualities are needed in a Stig?

"Silence, obviously. And being able to drive really really fast."

"And knowing zero about ducks."

"Right"

"Still friends with Clarkson?"

"I hope so. I think so. I've not seen him since the big fight in the high court… I have a lot of respect for Jeremy. He's very bright. I love the way he writes. He is really funny… But all the bullshit aside I think if they were to walk in right now, we'd all laugh and get really drunk."
Check out Bencollins.com for more info.

A Few Rounds with Vladimir Klitschko

It is an aggressive Thursday—the kind you'd love to punch in the nose. But you can't get past its left jab. You're swinging at air. The absurd clouds hang limp, bruised purple as if by Dr.

Steelhammer himself. The road! The highway is torn to hell for 100 kilometres and I'm sitting there with my tooth throbbing. We are going to be late and the unutterable senselessness of the task at hand (tinged with paranoia) shoots through me from head to toe like a hideous Michael Bolton high note.

I am struggling with me—my own worst enemy. It's a bad day. Please don't take my picture. I'm no champ, just another chump chasing newsprint. And yet… and yet… something outrageous was needed to pull me from my funk. An attack of vampire bats? A chase through the winding countryside pursued by a maniacal TIR driver? Half a dozen Margaritas, shaken not stirred? That's what the doctor ordered. Time to forget pain and suck it up, baby.

Far be it from me to cast aspersions—I happen to keep a bag of aspersions handy for such occasions—at the Polish highway system, but the atmosphere in the Audi was tense and dispiriting. Amy Winehouse supplied a suitable soundtrack as we crawled into the malignant late afternoon.

We were late, and I was scheduled to go ten rounds in Wroclaw with the heavyweight champ of the world, Vladimir Klitschko aka Dr. Steelhammer. His brother, the behemoth, Vitali, aka Dr Ironfist, who strides the ring like a Colossus (because he is one) would be boxing in two days against the hopeful Pole, Tomasz Adamek.

My jaw was throbbing, and I hadn't even begun the interview.

"What's the name of the place where we are meeting them?' I asked

Wojtek the photographer, a good man.

"Novocaine," he says.

"Are you shitting me?"

"No dude. For real."

Round 1

A writer, like a boxer, must prepare. So, I have watched an advance copy of the new biopic about boxing's first family several times. It's called Klitschko and it's fascinating. You don't have to like boxing to enjoy this film. It is rags to riches, East to West, triumph over adversity. It's grace under pressure from start to finish. If you wrote the script as fiction, people would call it too far-fetched. And yet the story arc is as compelling as any you might find in the annals of sport.

Of the film VK says, "This is a story of how two boys had dreams and how they've been working to make these dreams come true. In this documentary you can also see parts of our lives because boxing is not all of our lives, thank God. You also can get some stories behind the ropes or for some boxing fans you can take a look behind the scenes, not only what you guys see in the ring but also what's happening before entering the ring."

So, who are these guys? Huge automatons, emotionless yet effective? Terminators cooked up in some mad scientist's laboratory.

Many are suggesting that the heavyweight category is getting too… er… heavy, and that the Klitschko's need to be in a super category all their own with other big fighters (as in martial arts). Perhaps. But one should note that big boxers have been taken down by smaller fighters many times in the annals of boxing. There is no substitute for strategy and dedication. I would suggest that what makes VK so special, apart from the above, is his reach, yet at 206 cm his reach is still 2 cm less than that of George Foreman, whom Ali beat. "The harder they come, the harder they fall," as the great reggae man, Jimmy Cliff, sang. In fact, Foreman is the modern heavyweight who comes closest to the size of Vladimir. Ali had a reach of 203 cm.

If anything, they are performers, in the truest sense of the word. Performance is their watchword, both in and out of the ring. They are always in each other's corner. They think. They fight. They win. They are gentlemen in an age that hardly recognizes the meaning of the word. The Klitschko Brothers are a phenomenon unlike any ever seen in heavyweight boxing.

Two huge fighters who can jab and punch with anyone. But be sure: they have lost fights, Vladimir three, Vitali two. So, they can be beaten. As they say, it's not all about size. Sometimes it's the motion of the ocean.

So, what is all the whining about? Let's start with Spike Lee, with whom the Klitschko documentary producer, Leopold Hoesch, met to discuss directing the film. Spike Lee said he didn't believe the story deserved his attention because there just aren't that many good heavy-weights around to challenge those Ukrainian giants. A comment which seems at face value not only ridiculous but laughably prejudiced. If white people can revere black boxers, then why shouldn't the reverse be true? Rocky Marciano, the great boxer of the 1950s, retired undefeated after beating all the best black boxers of his generation. He had a reach of 170 cm and stood 180cm tall. Marciano consistently beat taller Black fighters with longer reaches: Jersey Joe Walcott (188cm), Ezzard Charles (185cm), Archie Moore (191cm) and even his childhood hero, Joe Louis (190cm). I hope for Mr. Lee's sake my point is made. Beyond that, should you wish to talk about growing up "rough," imagine growing up in So-viet Russia [the Soviet Union? - they're Ukrainian] living in one room with your mother, father, brother, sister and grandmother. Imagine being within close range when Chernobyl blew up. Imagine… well you get the point. All I'm saying is that if growing up tough makes great boxers then the Ks can fall right into line with anybody. By contrast, Ali grew up in comfort in Louisville, despite the racial prejudice. In the Soviet Union everyone was 'ghetto,' if you will, except the higher-up party officials.

Back to now. Between them they hold all the major belts in box-ing, an unparalleled achievement. How in the world could this happen? Their new film, Klitschko, explores the history of these two brothers, who are less like Kane and Abel than like twins, despite their five-year gap in age. In fact, early on in their career Vladimir once filled in for an injured Vitali in a German fight with no one the wiser. Germany embraces them as America finally embraced Ali. Two Slavs as kings of the German boxing world. The wheel turns. Max Schmeling must have loved the inescapable irony.

Who is the more outstanding pugilist? Each dubs the other king. Style? Vitali is a classic counter- puncher in the mould of Marvin Hagler, Evander Holyfield and Max Schmeling (who was a close per-sonal friend), while Vladimir is a careful stylist who reads the other fighter using jabs to wear him down, reminiscent of Larry Holmes, Sug-ar Ray Leonard and the Greatest, Muhammad Ali.

These guys don't float like a butterfly or sting like a bee. They glide like panthers and maul like a bear.

Despite constant criticism from commentators and boxers alike, for being 'unexciting,' no one says the Ks are not effective. The record serves. VK, champ since 2006, has surpassed his brother's achievements by quietly becoming the seventh longest reigning heavyweight in history, just ahead of Ali and only a year and a half away from being second to Joe Louis, who held the title for nearly 12 years. It's curious but VK looks bigger further away than he does close up. You get the contrast in size between him and everyone else when he enters the room. But up close his size is not so overwhelming, at least not when sitting safely on a sofa in the Wroclaw club. Everyone looks bigger in the ring, even the little guys. People say to him all the time he doesn't look that big and he says, "Wait till I take my shirt off."

I feel so unprepared for this interview that it's embarrassing. It was a last- minute thing. I haven't watched nearly enough fight film, but then this is not to be a piece of esoterica.

WRR: How's it going champ?

VK: I'm having a great time in Wroclaw. It's such a beautiful city with beautiful people. I just arrived yesterday, and I have seen how the city is full of culture and beautiful streets and buildings.. . I used to fight in Warsaw.

He hasn't been in Poland for like 15 years since he and Vitali used to work out with Saleta, the former European champion.

WRR: So, who's going to win the fight on Saturday?

VK: It's going to be an interesting fight. My brother is going to win the fight because he knows what

to expect. He knows the way Tomasz fights, and that he is a serious fighter who has been champion at two different weight classes. And he has proved himself in the heavyweight division against even taller guys like Michael Grant (August 2010 unanimous decision). It's going to be a really tough fight, and Tomasz is going to reach a peak of energy from the nation watching him and being at home. But I'm more than sure that Vitali is going to win and the sooner the better for me because I'm going to be in his corner.

Round 3

WRR: You are always in each other's corner. I watched the film three times.

VK: How did you like it?

WRR: It was great.

VK: Why are you saying that?

WRR: I'm saying that because there's nowhere for me to run right now. No, seriously I'm saying that because it's moving because of the family story, plus you get some great commentary from the other boxers that you've fought. Lennox Lewis for example. There are very few films which have boxers really talking so eloquently about boxing and giving such an in-depth look at their whole life, not just their life in the ring.

VK: I'm glad you liked it.

Round 4

We are running on truly little time: thirty minutes for an interview when we were promised ninety. And there are photos to take, so I take time between rounds briefly to explain who I am and what kind of piece I'm writing for Malemen and what kind of magazine it is.

VK: Mail man? That's like the mailman. The guy who brings the mail?

WRR: Not really. It's Male and Men. It's tautological. Repetitious?

VK: Oh yeah. I see. I know what tautology means. (Laughs, thank God. I feel like Howard Cosell interviewing Foreman or Ali, only without the toupee.)

WRR: They could have called it 'Femalemen'... but then we'd both have to be wearing dresses.

VK: You know what? I'm very excited about this interview because you are not a typical interview guy. You are going to do the kind of questions to see who I am. I'm looking at your system that you have there and it's very logical. (My notebook is open on my lap with a diagram of the things I want to talk about.)

WRR: Oh, you see that. It's called a mind map.

VK: Sure, I get it. It's good. You know what? You should actually print a picture of this. I think it's really cool. People are usually very standard. You're getting an interview and the guys are asking standard questions. But this is interesting for the people who are going to read the article to see your plan.

WRR: Thanks. You know there is so much to talk about and usually I would spend more time with the person I'm talking to, but we'll do the best we can, and so far, I think we are getting somewhere different... There was one thing I was particularly interested in, not about boxing.

Where was the place you grew up exactly? I'm asking because of the Chernobyl section in the film and how that event affected your family very directly.

VK: I was born in Kazakhstan. Have you heard about the nuclear weapons tests underground in Kazakhstan? The same thing as in Nevada in the States. This was very close to the place where I was born and each time when there was an explosion there was an earthquake. So, I was born there, and after the first grade of school we moved because of my father (a military man) to Prague. And then in 1986 we went to Kiev.

(Scanning through my brain: I went to school in Atlanta, and he won an Olympic Gold medal there in 1996.)

WRR: In the film you talk about being a kid playing in radioactive water. Where was that? (Mind your manners. Don't go there with the radioactive joke about how he grew so big.)

Round 5

VK: Right, when the explosion happened in Chernobyl on 26th April 1986 my father was in charge of all the helicopters which were flying over the plant and dropping a certain substance (sand, lead, clay and boron) that absorbed the radiation. There were cars and trucks and helicopters that had been flying back and forth, and it was very important to wash them out. I remember that it was warm and all the water that had been washed out of those vehicles was in puddles. So, we were there in a military airport near Kiev, and this was where the helicopters were landing, and the cars and trucks were being cleaned.

WRR: I visited Chernobyl.

VK: Where were you?

WRR: Chernobyl town and…

VK: Were you in zone 1?

WRR: Yeah, I went straight to the reactor. The French were still working on the sarcophagus to cover the whole thing.

VK: I was there two weeks ago. Did you go to the schools and the kindergarten?

WRR: Yeah, we went everywhere they would let us go. We got to walk around Pripyat and see the Ferris wheel.

VK: Did you have a radiation meter?

WRR: Sure, the whole time.

Round 6

WRR: Obviously that was a foundation experience, and your father has had cancer associated with his participation in the clean-up. Just how important has your family been in what you have achieved? This is a central part of the new film of course. Do you think you could have done what you've done without your brother and the family support you've had?

VK: Never. Because I would never have started boxing without my brother. He is a fighter. He was born with it in his bones. I became a fighter because I always wanted to be like my brother. As a kid I always wanted to do what my brother did. As the youngest you know. My father was always away at work. My Mom of course wasn't interested in boxing. So next to me all the time was this five years older brother. I just wanted to do whatever he wanted to do. I started with wrestling, then judo and then some kickboxing and somehow boxing because of my brother. My first dream was to be a doctor.

WRR: What's the special connection apart from your brother being older and wanting to compete with him and to some extent emulate him? What have you learned from boxing?

VK: I have learned a lot. Through boxing and through sport I got into the best university in the world and got the best education you can get. I got to travel a lot. That means I got to know different mentalities. I got to know different languages. I got to know different cultures. I got to know people from different fields from journalists to all kinds of people like the Dalai Lama and famous boxers.

WRR: Muhammad Ali?

VK: I got to meet him, yes. I also met Putin and Clinton, for example.

WRR: Who is someone you look up to besides your brother or your father or mother?

VK: I really try to take the best of every person because there was never anyone, I felt 100% I had to meet...

WRR: What about Ali? Was he impressive?

VK: Yes, unfortunately he is not able to communicate like he used to, but the communication still worked pretty good because I'm into doing magic, and he is too. So, we showed each other magic tricks and performed them for each other.

WRR: What trick did you show him, and what did he show you?

VK: I gave him the trick about thought-reading. Somebody writes down on a card their thought and then you guess it exactly. And he taught me Three-card Monte. He was something... but if you want to talk about famous personalities the Dalai Lama was very impressive to me. I met him and talked to him. Clinton and Putin were very impressive. Two different perspectives on life, two different continents and backgrounds. I met Clinton twice, actually, and really had enough time to talk to him and I learned a lot, asked a lot of questions that were interesting to me.

Round 7

WRR: What did you ask Clinton?

VK: I asked him how he can win over people of a country when they don't understand even the language that he speaks. The first time I met him was in Germany and the second time in Ukraine where he had a speech. People were cheering him like a rock star. People were really loving him. They could read the lines of what he was saying on a big screen, but he has such charisma and such good will and such a way of communicating with people that I asked him how he does it, what his secret was? And he said that there is no secret. You have to be well-prepared. Politicians can't afford to make mistakes, just as there is a scientific language there is a language of politics. Trying to sound smart is actually not smart because you have to attend to the audience and understand who are they, where are they coming from and you have to talk in their language, use uncomplicated words so they can understand you well. Even if it's in English in the States and you give a speech and it sounds smart, but people don't understand you then you aren't much of a politician. People will say this guy is smart, but I'm not really getting what he said. So, if you talk in a way that people will understand then they will really accept you and follow you.

WRR: So, are you going into Ukrainian politics like your brother?

VK: I was just wondering you know. I've made a lot of speeches and right now I'm not involved in it directly like Vitali, who has his own political party in Ukraine. I was involved in the Orange Revolution, but now I'm not doing it as actively as Vitali... but talking about celebrity... There are many people who are unknown who give me knowledge and wisdom. There is a woman who cleans the floor at a restaurant where I go, and some of the things she says are so logical and wise. So, let's not put too much faith in celebrity. Everyone looks up to celebrity. And of course, people should be given credit for doing things well, but there are plenty of unknown people who are amazing.

WRR: We, me and Wojtek, were just talking about that driving down here.

VK: Yeah, it's true.

WRR: We were talking about musicians and saying how many great ones there are that no one knows about.

VK: You are so right. I have a friend of mine who has the best voice ever. Seriously. The strongest. The best. Everything. But he doesn't know how to manage things. Still, I think he is the most talented guy. I mean I've heard a lot of singers. Believe me this guy is very special, and he performs but it's not his job. He's actually a priest in a church. And his voice is amazing. But he is not selling copies of his songs or anything like that or signing a contract with one of the music labels. Yet his voice is unbelievable. Un-be-Liev-able.

WRR: Excellent stuff. But I'd like to switch topics on you back to boxing if I may. Since we don't have much time.

VK: Sure.

Round 7

WRR: What's the toughest fight you ever had?

VK: They are all tough. But the toughest fight is the one you are going to lose. You too. It's the fight with yourself. There is no opponent that is tougher than you. If you are going to fight yourself then you have already lost. You don't want to get involved with fighting yourself, if you understand what I'm talking about.

WRR: Yes, I do.

VK: I think all of us do, really. And at certain times we fight with ourselves and it's really tough to overcome yourself. You can't win if you're fighting yourself.

WRR: What about in the ring?

VK: In the ring it's the same thing. When you're exhausted or, say, you've torn your biceps or something, and you are struggling. It's already a fight with yourself, and you have to say, 'I cannot give up.' You may be damaged, but you can't show your opponent that you are hurt. I have a friend who works with lions, and of course the lion is much stronger, but he leads the lion with his voice and makes the lion believe he is in charge. Even one time when the lion had injured him, he didn't let the lion know.

WRR: So, we have to conceal our weaknesses in battle. So how did you feel when your brother was in that epic battle with Lennox Lewis (the great British heavyweight)?

VK: I felt it was Vitali's chance, just like it is Adamek's chance on Saturday night. Vitali was even better than he had ever been before in that fight. He just did everything that he needed to do and even if it was very difficult with the injury he had (a horrific deep cut over his left eye) he was fighting like a lion. It was tough to watch. I was right there. I was on the left side of his corner and his left eye was very badly cut. I understood that there were two sides of me: that I could throw in the towel to stop the fight. But then, okay, Vitali was winning the fight, so let's give it a try. It's very difficult to send him back knowing that I could also stop the fight at any time. It was a very tough decision not to stop it and to let him keep fighting.

(The ringside doctor Paul Wallace later explained his decision to stop the fight: 'When he raised his head up, his upper eyelid covered his field of vision. At that point I had no other option but to stop the fight. If he had to move his head to see me, there was no way he could defend his way against a punch.')

Round 8

WRR: In 1975 Norman Mailer wrote a book called 'The Fight' about the Ali-Foreman fight in Zaire in which he compares Ali's tactics in winning the fight to a chess match. Watching the new documentary about you and Vitali, I noticed that you and your brother not only play chess, but you have also compared your own boxing style to playing chess. I have a friend who was a child prodigy in chess in the US and I asked him about this and he said (reading): 'It's all about staying a move ahead and making your opponent think he has you, the best games are where your opponent makes a great plan and suddenly finds himself in a losing position, because like in Aikido or any martial art you use your opponent's energy against him.' So, what are the similarities between chess and boxing in your mind?

VK: There is a good saying in chess that compares to boxing. 'To see what they see, then seek what they seek.' So, when you prepare for the match, you are obviously watching your opponent. So, you are studying him. It's not that complicated. Everyone has an ability to fight in a certain way. It's very predictable. You just study and you are 100%

ready for the fight, and you know what to expect. You know the punches, the body movements. You calculate everything. And you watch your own fights to see yourself through the eyes of your opponent. You ask questions from the people in your team about what you would do if you were the other guy. You get all these ideas and put them together to decide what you are going to do. That's why it is so comparable to chess. To see what they see, seek what they seek, so when you switch the board around, you are going to get a totally different view of the pieces that are on the board. That's seems simple but that's how it works.

WRR: I can see we are running out of time. But can I ask you this? Where do you rate yourselves in the ranks of great heavyweights?

VK: Nowhere. Really nowhere. I want to give respect to legacy. I think Vitali and I will just enjoy the time we have in boxing. It's an exciting life. We don't decide where we are. You decide.

I never told him about my toothache. Writers have to learn to play with pain, just like boxers. Unfortunately, I only made it eight rounds instead of the scheduled ten.

A Matter of Life and Breath:
Aneta Kopacz, Film Director

L ife sometimes comes too early, and death always comes too soon. In her third decade on our planet, Aneta Kopacz somehow finds herself a specialist in life and death, a seasoned jouster with the ultimate questions. Her short documentary film, Joanna, about a young mother dying of cancer, was nominated for an Oscar (2013) and tapped to win by the Hollywood Reporter. Though it did not win, the story of a thirty-something cancer patient coming to terms with death on camera was terrifyingly riveting. In this arresting film, which is more about life than death in its being aware of one's demise, there were echoes of renowned author Christopher Hitchens, who also died of cancer of the oesophagus, the ultimate irony since he was perhaps the ablest debater of our time. Hitchens, too, died publicly and courageously. So, it can be done, dying with dignity, in this often-graceless age. Ms. Kopacz graduated in psychology, an appropriate grounding for her recent livelihood, from the University of Warsaw, and then took a postgraduate course in reporting before studying filmmaking at the Andrzej Wajda School in Krakow.

Her latest project is an ambitious TV serial for Polish TVP. My 600 Grams is an intense study of how premature birth affects families. It's filmed on location in a hospital in Krakow where Miss Kopacz struggles to master her task along with the emotions of the mothers and fathers whose children arrive too soon for their own good.

Today is a warm, sunny day and we are sitting outside of the main studio of Polish Television. A band is warming up too, for a show to introduce new programs for the 2015-16 television season. The prevalent song is All You Need Is Love... and a good doctor, the thought occurs.

WRR: Why this subject and why now?

AK: I was chosen to do this by the producer (from Polish TVP).

121

One day he just called me because of Joanna. People connect me to tough stuff and that I'm willing to do these subjects that are about illness.

WRR: They think. What do you think? Why do you do it?

AK: I don't know. I'm tired of it. She will soon wrap up shooting.

WRR: But really?

AK: Somehow, I like to take on things that are impossible to do. Because this project now is impossible to do really. Because you cannot just enter the hospital and go to the intensive care unit where some of the babies are dying. Where there is huge stress for doctors and for parents. Emotions are very, very high most of the time. So, imagine the cameras there shooting people crying and in distress. During the first two weeks it was not clear we would be able to do this. We were seen as enemies by the hospital. So, they tried to get rid of us. We are saving lives. You are not welcome. We were in the way. So, it was really hard work to convince them that we were not interested in filming the procedures. With checking them, looking over their shoulder. Seeing if they are okay with every step.

WRR: They were worried about you documenting their mistakes rather than…

AK: Yes, yes. Or parents crying and we would shoot them very closely when a kid is dying. They didn't trust us.

WRR: Is that in the show.

AK: Yes, but we are not close to this. We are outside shooting discreetly. We need to show that kids are dying because if not, then people will not believe us. We have to show that sometimes they don't make it and all aspects. So also, kids dying.

WRR: What did you learn in your previous film that is helping you in doing this one?

AK: I'm not sure if I learned anything that helped me now, but the most important thing in every documentary is to have a strong relationship to the subject. You have to give and take. You have to share your life, share your opinion and then you can get into a relationship and exchange information. In this case we are doing everything online. We are shooting and trying to create a relationship with people. Imagine. Normally when everything is ok, then the mother is the first person holding the child. In this case the situation is totally different. Most of the time, the mother is in very bad shape after giving birth. In this case she can only see the child for a moment and then the doctors take the child and put it in the incubator to save its life. When they come out, I don't know how to say it…

WRR: born...

AK: When they are born, the mother has only a moment, and then a lot of people are saving the kid's life. They take the kid away for this intensive care and it's often twenty-four hours before the mother can see her kid for the real first time. Just after the birth, I can meet a man standing by intensive care, and I'm sure this is the father. So, then I try to convince him: Listen we were shooting when your wife was giving birth. So, we were there, and now for the first time in a few minutes you are going to see your kid for the first time.

Can we be with you? The answer: incubators use oxygen supplementation by head hood or nasal cannula, or even continuous positive airway pressure (CPAP). Infant respiratory distress syndrome is the leading cause of death in preterm infants. The main treatments is CPAP, in addition to administering pulmonary surfactant and stabilizing the blood sugar, blood salts, and blood pressure. Of course, no. But it's our moment, our intimacy. So, our task is to convince him that this will be a great moment to have documented.

WRR: Does almost everyone say, no?

AK: Nobody says yes right away.

WRR: How does this intrusion affect you?

AK: I feel really bad. I shouldn't be talking to this guy. Just leave him alone. But I try to persuade him, nonetheless.

WRR: Why is it important to do this story in such an intensive way? There is an undeniable voyeuristic aspect. You are filming around a life-and-death situation. Not a combat situation where the parties are complicit but an accidental situation involving the most innocent of participants. How do you get yourself in the right mind to do this?

AK: I'm really very interested in people and really like to talk to them, and perhaps I have some ability to get to know people quickly. I'm also a psychologist. So, I try to help them. The parents have no idea what to do in this situation. But I have experience from being there before them. So, I explain to them they have to disinfect their hands and how they have to wear their protective clothes. You have to wear the hat like this. I will help you.

WRR: You are becoming involved.

AK: Yes, and I help them a lot. I'm the one who is next to them very intensively at the moment they are completely alone... So, it's: Give me a chance. Let's try. Slowly, step by step, they agree to do it. Another difficult step is when they bring their wives and they are very weak, and they don't want to be filmed. Please don't shoot me because I look awful. But this is the exact shot I need. Tomorrow will be too late. This is the first time you see your child. Sometimes they agree and sometimes they say no.

WRR: It occurs to me that this is rather like a reality hospital show. Some people might criticize this as exploitation, but on the other hand this is a very serious problem with one in ten children being born prematurely. So, there is this balance between invading privacy and illuminating the problem. Was it like this with the cancer movie?

AK: After Joanna people told me that I changed their life with that movie. Joanna is not about cancer, it's about life. One girl told me, you know what, I was wondering if I should have a child, but now I want to have one more than anything because it is a purpose in itself. Or for example some guy says, I was quarrelling with my wife, and this was so stupid. Life is so short. It is banal, but suddenly I realize that people need reminding about this constantly. You can see them change their priorities. People see that they need to change their way of thinking. It seems so obvious.

WRR: How old was Joanna?

AK: 36.

WRR: So, in that movie you were showing the end and here you are showing the beginning. It's a tough journey with rocky starts and endings.

AK: That's right. That's why mostly I want to say to people start to appreciate what you have. It is so simple.

WRR: It can all go away very easily.

AK: And you know what? I think that for me the most important things in life are the banal, the ordinary.

WRR: You have your own children?

AK: Yes, a daughter, four.

WRR: Did you always know what you wanted to be when you grew up?

AK: I had some idea. But you know what? People kept talking to me and saying: I know what I want to do in my life but I'm still waiting for a better time. How can you be sure there will be a time in the future? Start now I say. But people wait. They think: Now I can't be brave enough to do what I really think. They settle for less. You really need to be brave to realize your dreams. Because they think the world will end if they fail. So, it's better not to try. It's banal but I love that. It's so simple. Start appreciating what you have now and start realizing your dreams. Do it now. Don't wait!".

The Poet of the Sandinistas

It would probably be appropriate to say that Carlos Mejia Godoy wrote the soundtrack of the Sandinista movement. So, let's say it.

This is how. The year is 1974. Daniel Ortega, their iconic leader, along with other key Sandinista leaders, all languish in a Managua prison.

It has been nearly two years since a massive earthquake devastated the city, yet few realize that an even bigger shake-up is ahead.

Prison authorities grant a special favour to the Sandinista leader, Ortega, so that Carlos Mejia Godoy, a popular radio personality, can come to perform for the prison population. Carlos had started his career as a so-called Corporito on the radio station Radio Corporacion, on which he sang his own songs each day ridiculing politicians and political parties. His sardonic lyrics were especially incendiary to the populace at large, held as they were in thrall to the hated dictator, Somoza.

He was put in jail for a little while in 1974-5. He was friends with the wife of Ortega. He hung out with her.

He was not politically active as such. His connection was as an artist. When they killed Chamorra in Managua, owner of La Prensa, they sent CMG to Europe, to Spain, and that's where he became an international star with regional music from Nicaragua… They didn't know he was a Sandinista in Spain.

Somoza was a piece of work, a real so and so, so disgusting he used to have political enemies thrown into the Massa volcano. He was so repugnant that even the US government disowned him in the end. He was a dirty punk who was so brazen that he even cheated Howard Hughes.

The warden agrees to the visit, but orders "no political songs." The day of the concert comes. All the prisoners march in for the show—except for the rebellious Sandinistas.True to form the warden has gone back on his word. Nevertheless, Carlos plays the concert, saying to himself, I will pass by the cell of my comrades when we leave to give them the thumbs up. And indeed, on leaving he did pass by the Sandinistas, who were isolated from the rest of the prisoners, in brilliant sunshine in the yard below.

"Carlos! Play us a little something," shouted out Ortega and his comrades.

So, Carlos stopped and sang his recent hit to them from the window. The song was María de los guardias, a recent song and one of his most popular pieces. It had been a huge hit in Spain and Mexico.

Carlos remembers: "When his mother visited Daniel in prison, he used to give her long, long letters in almost invisible writing on tiny pieces of paper. She hid the writing paper in the loaves of fresh bread she brought him. The prison guards didn't check her on the way out. She would hide the letters in the heel of her shoe—the heel would come off and she would hide them there. Like a diamond smuggler.

The letters contained some poems that Carlos would use as lyrics in his songs.

Now on a hot and humid Saturday afternoon decades later, I am sitting with Carlos Mejia Godoy— Carlos, he asks me to call him—at La Casa de los Mejia Godoy (The House of the Mejia Godoy), his music venue and restaurant across the street from the Crowne Plaza Hotel in downtown Managua.

This hot and sticky Saturday just happens to be the birthday of the revolution's namesake, Augusto Sandino, the Pancho Villa figure of Nicaragua. The previous night, Don Carlos had performed a three-hour concert for a packed house at his venue.

Carlos is not only the most popular artist in Nicaragua, these days he is also a revered political figure. His old comrade, Daniel Ortega, has been president since 2007 following his first term as President from 1989 to 1990. What does all this politics have to do with art? In Nicaragua, the two things are inseparable.

Born in 1943 in the northern hills near the Honduran border in Somoto, Carlos came from a musical family. Indeed, his father wanted all of his sons to be musicians.

"My father was a great musician. He would have been famous if he had gone to the city." Their father gave his talented sons a love for their region's music, surprisingly based on local versions of the waltz, polka and even the mazurka. Carlos learned to play the guitar and accordion.

"Oh yes," Carlos says, "I wanted to be Bernstein or Toscanini conducting a symphony." Instead he ended up being more influenced by the American folk tradition of Bob Dylan and Pete Seeger.

Don Carlos didn't go to music school though. He was just as fascinated by the overall culture of his country as he was by its music.

Eventually he migrated from acting and broadcasting—he spent his apprenticeship in the mid-1960s working in German television—into song writing, where he made his first big impact when one of his songs stole the show at a Latin American song festival in Costa Rica in 1970.

Notoriety followed on his return to Nicaragua, where he made a radio program called Corporito, which earned both public favour and government scorn. The program took a courageously critical view of the Somoza dictatorship, especially after the 1970 murder of prominent union officials.

"Somoza was outrageous, and I was constantly in trouble," he says. "Being fined and having my life threatened were normal events."

The earthquake which struck Managua in December 1972, killing 10,000 people, was a psychic as well as seismic disturbance, according to Don Carlos.

Later relief efforts shone a spotlight on the corruption of the Somoza regime, which was widely accused of pocketing aid money donated for rebuilding the city, including some raised by a Rolling Stones charity concert. To date the city has yet to fully recover. The cathedral, which was designed and built in Belgium and reassembled in Managua in 1920, is still a pathetic ruin.

Don Carlos was on the sixth floor of the broadcasting building downtown editing a Christmas program when the first tremors came.

"Somoza's radio was on fourth floor," he says. "My wife, who was with me in the editing suite, immediately said "Let's go!" So, we drove to our house ten kilometres away. When the earthquake was finally over, we couldn't get out of our house. The doors were all jammed! But our neighbours came to the rescue. They were shouting, 'We must save Corporito!' That was what they called me because of my radio program."

Next day's news revealed the grim reality. The broadcasting building had been completely destroyed, killing all those who had remained within. The centre of the city had collapsed as if bombed into oblivion.

In the chaos of the ensuing years, leading to Somoza's escape in 1979 (so oddly similar to Batista's flight from Cuba in 1959), Don Carlos used the weapon of song to aid the Sandinista guerrillas. His songs satirized the government while sympathizing with ordinary people and their desultory way of life.

"Nicaragua is everything you see and hear. Its geography, its wildlife, its landscapes, its sense of humour and even our love of gossip," Don Carlos says.

He was inspired by his people's endurance against crippling and cruel oppression. "The people were up in arms... I felt no alternative. I had to try and help... It was more of a feeling than a conscious political thought with me."

In the seventies his songs captured the imagination of millions around the world and earned him honours for Best Group and Best Song as well as a gold record in Spain in 1977 for El son nuestro de cada dia.

In 1979 he had another gold disc in Spain for La misa campesina. Meanwhile he had earned a name as the poetic voice of the Sandinista revolution. When the excellent film Under Fire came out in 1983 starring Gene Hackman and Nick Nolte as journalists during the last days of the Nicaraguan revolution, it was Carlos Mejia Godoy's revolutionary anthem that played as the film credits rolled.

In present day Nicaragua one hardly associates Don Carlos or even Daniel Ortega himself with the now hardly palpable revolutionary past. Nicaragua is a different country today, more self-assured, more open and despite often frightful continuing poverty, more relaxed.

Yet the fire still burns. You have only to hear Carlos Mejia Godoy launch into his beautiful song Nicaragua, Nicaraguita to be swept up into his world. The lyric and the object of affection become one.

Oh Nicaragua Nicaraguita
The most beautiful flower dearest to my heart
The hero and martyr Diriangen
Died for you Nicaraguita
Oh, Nicaragua you are even sweeter
Than the honey from Tamagas
But now that you are free Nicaraguita
I love you much more
But now that you are free Nicaraguita
I love you much more

John Lydon: International Treasure

The year is 1976. Something is happening in London that no one understands. The bicentennial year of the American Revolution was a good time for marking rebellion. The UK is in a state of emotional anarchy with young people across the country searching desperately for answers to a situation that doesn't seem to work. Working class youth across the country are stuck on the dole and looking for a way out of dead-end factory jobs, something, anything, with a bit more glamour that promises a way out.

A nineteen-year-old named John Lydon, soon to be "Johnny Rotten," frequents a clothes shop owned by Malcolm McLaren in the Kings Road. McLaren is thinking about putting a band together and he likes the young man's style: a combination of spikey dyed-orange hair and clothes stuck together with safety pins combined with a snarling sense of humor and a singing voice better described as a howl. The Sex Pistols took aim at the Establishment and blazed away.

It seems to fit the moment.

Enter the cabaret show starring a working-class knight errant tilting at windbags instead of windmills—a split personality parlaying his own dual nature into a marvelously self-aware character, equal halves dreaming Don Quixote and salt-of-the-earth Sancho Panza. But with plenty of "bollocks."

By 1978 they were through. The Sex Pistols and other bands had led a revolution that changed the music scene forever, prompting prominent rock figures like Neil Young to wonder if they had been made irrelevant. Young's seminal song, Hey, Hey, My, My as an expression of this self-doubt.

"Is this the story of Johnny Rotten?" sang Young as his contemporaries worried, they were becoming obsolete. The death of Elvis that same year seemed to sound a death knell for rock, as The Clash (whom Lydon finds to be pale imitators cried, "No Elvis, Beatles or Rolling Stones in 1977!"

Fast-forward to 2016.

The same young rebel who snarled about "anarchy" and "the fascist regime" is now 30-years married, has 30,000 dollars' worth of dental work (he was called "Rotten" because of his terrible teeth) and is a solid citizen of Malibu, California, who drives a Volvo ("because me and Nora are sensible").

It is precisely 11 AM in Los Angeles when the call goes through.

There is a kind of mini roar on the line followed by "Okaaaaaay."

"Are you there?" I challenge the voice from the other side.

"Yes, it lives!" Mr. Lydon refers to himself in the impersonal pronoun. Punk is not dead.

It is early in the day for rock and roll.

"I've been up since seven, but I haven't really woken up yet. Around midday is when I really get rockin'. Been doing interviews all morning. I don't mind doing that at all… No harm in talking.

Is this for internet?"

"No, it's for print," I say.

"The written word on paper. Well, you've already got my support and attention immediately… But that doesn't mean I'm going to reveal all my secrets."

"Well, this is a good place to do it. By the way I bring you greetings from the Godfather of Polish punk and reggae, Robert Brylewski."

"Oh my gosh," says Lydon in his unmistakable Cockney twang. "It's funny isn't it how reggae has crept into every culture round the world in very intriguing ways. I grew up with reggae. It was always in my neighborhood so it's part of my bloodstream really. When I hear it's taken root in odd places like Poland my automatic attitude is all right, hey, fucking thieves."

He laughs. "So long as the subject matter is something that affects Polish people, then it seems fine. They've found a backbeat to the voice."

"It may be better to burn out than to fade away" but Lydon is a survivor. He outlived the comet-trajectory of the Sex Pistols and moved on. The band famously broke up at a gig in San Francisco in 1978 when Lydon exited stage left mid-concert saying, "Ever felt like you've been cheated?" The documentary about the Sex Pistols, The Great Rock and Roll Swindle followed in 1979, telling the story of their epic crash and burn.

Lydon refused to do that. He survived the band as Sid Vicious did not. He died of a heroin overdose in New York in February 1979, soon after being accused of stabbing his girlfriend to death. Lydon had risen and founded his new band: Public Image Ltd. Luck was good to him and played a part in his survival to today. In 1988, he and his wife, Nora, were supposed to fly to New York on Pan Am flight 103 that crashed in Lockerbie, Scotland. They missed the flight. Nora was late with the packing.

He has always been a commentator. Musing on politics keeps him feeling frisky.

Says Lydon, "The Occupy Wall Street movement had everyone involved in it. I think it's the best political movement in modern times because of its unity of different groups. They found one consensus that Wall Street is to blame for a lot of things. There's always money at the bottom of it if its America. Just follow the dollar bill signs."

He takes a pause to light a cigarette (Marlboro Red).

"You still smoke?" I ask. "Smokers are a dying breed. I quit. I feel like I quit heroin. Because it's supposed to be harder to stop. So, I feel like I quit heroin too."

He laughs. "That's a good one. No future in that. That's a dead-end career in heroin. Hasn't ended up well for anyone. And it never will because it's the kind of drug you use for an answer to your insecurities without realizing that self-doubt is a wonderful part of your personality. You must leave yourself open to question. Not only from yourself, which is obviously your biggest challenge, but for every one of us. Once you understand that you find that those kinds of chemicals are unimportant. Irrelevant dangerous, stupid, foolish, and expensive."

"And it destroys relationships. Do you know about the 27 club?"

"I don't know about that," says Lydon.

"You know people who die at the age of 27 like Jim Morrison, Kurt Cobain, Jimi Hendrix, Amy Winehouse. There are a whole lot of them."

"They call it the 27 club? That's an oddity. It's not my kind of mathematical conclusion. That's roughly the age though in the music industry when people have to decide whether they are going to exist for the rest of their lives and give up trying to pretend they are still sixteen and accept what adulthood holds. That is usually where the drug problems come in their hardest and fastest. It's the fear of the unknown. The fear of growing old and dilapidated. I'm now 60. I went through a similar anxiety in my twenties. I thought that's going to be the end of my life. I'd never be taken seriously again because I'd be just another old fart. That was the real turning point and also the transition between Pistols and PIL so there were many, many emotional and mental and physical problems going on all at once. But I pulled through it, and I've got to say amphetamine kind of helped at that time."

He laughs.

There is more to that story. Lydon is terrified of deep sleep because when he was seven years old he had meningitis, resulting in a coma for several months. When he revived, he had "no memory of anything or anybody."

"It took something like four years to get my complete memory back. And so, anything like sleeping pills or anything like that that knocks me out terrifies me. I'm constantly aware of the possibility of not waking up. Some of my worst nightmares are when I know I'm sound asleep and I want to be awake. I'm fighting within my own mind while I'm deeply asleep to wake myself up. It's an amazing battle of will… I can do it. I can master that part of my psyche because I practiced."

As a result, he has always put a premium consciousness. He sleeps little.

And you doesn't get tired?

"Yeah, oh terrible. And I don't care how old it makes me appear. I like my afternoon nap," he says with a laugh. He laughs readily and often, using laughter as a way to grease the wheels of conversation.

"You and Churchill," I say. "I knew I was going to get a comparison between you and Churchill into this piece." In 2002 Lydon was voted one of the 100 Greatest Britons in a UK poll (number 87, Churchill was number one).

Sleeplessness doesn't stop him writing songs. He compartmentalizes the ideas carefully in his mind long before he ever gets to writing them down. Song writing comes from emotion, he says. He may have a dozen ideas in his head at one time, carefully laid away until he is ready to commit to paper. He writes the words first and the music follows.

He describes his creative process as being similar to that of the late comedian, Robin Williams, "constantly throwing out ideas." He has a wicked sense of humor, for which he is famous, beneath that sometimes-earnest exterior. He has sometimes called the Sex Pistols, a kind of cabaret act.

"There's a lot of wisdom comes through in comedy. It's a very interesting part of the brain that resolves problems in comedic ways. By doing so you notice in the flaws in human thinking. It's a very important part of the personality to be open to humor.

"It is somewhat of a battle, but it's a bloody interesting one to be able to argue with yourself on a daily basis," he say. "For me the word comes first and then goes in search of emotional tones and notes to express that rant."

Perhaps his most well-known post-Pistols song is Rise, the first single from his PIL's fifth recording (Album, 1986). The song was written about apartheid in South Africa. "I may be wrong. I may be right. I may be black. I may be white," he wails.

"Yeah, that's questioning myself. It's really a collection of thoughts," he says.

He likes writing and he likes writers. James Joyce is a favorite. So is Oscar Wilde. Both are Irish and Lydon is of Irish Catholic heritage.

"Usually, the authors who come across the best contain wisdom, wit, irony and maybe satire… an in-depth analysis of the worst aspects of being a human being. The jealousy and envy, the hate, and the spite… They are all relevant. You can't say let's get rid of envy because it's important to go through all that thought process to come out the other end… I suppose the sheer mockery of Oscar Wilde on the British class system. As a young man, I found his attitudes on the class system to be really mind opening…"

One might say the same of John Lydon. Illuminating and shocking—back in the seventies. His song, God Save the Queen, a take on the pomp and ceremony of royalty in decline, was banned from the radio, a distinction he shares with one of his influences, John Lennon, whose song Cold Turkey about quitting heroin, was also banned. Only twice in the history of the UK charts was there no Number One.

He has always been known for his tough-minded and subversive wit: God Save the Queen. Anarchy for the UK. Pretty Vacant. New York. Knowing what we know now, it is hard to believe these songs were taken merely at face value.

"God save the Queen, for example, was me throwing down the gauntlet really. "Let's have a conversation on this, what have you got to offer?… But when I first started with the Pistols, I had to learn very soon that these TV hosts had to be dealt with. So, words became my weapons. And when I was met with aggression and hostility, I would reply in kind. But there is a lot more going on with me than just that. The situation demanded that kind of response. I wasn't going to sit there and be told I'm a moron because I come from the working class."

He distrusts politics in general. "I don't read political thought of one party or another. Because I find them to be very self-serving... Mind you I have a problem with the libertarian movement because I think we all have a responsibility to our fellow human beings. We have an obligation to look after each other. Just because a young child is from a poor background, it doesn't mean it doesn't deserve cancer treatment. This I don't owe anything to anybody is ludicrous because that puts us in the condition of wild beasts... Don't kick a man when he is down and don't view being wealthy as an act of God."

He considers the works of Charles Dickens to be part of his inheritance as a Londoner. Scrooge syndrome is far too prevalent in the world today. "For me that's part of my culture. To me that's for more valuable—the knowledge in those words—than having wealthy parents and driving a Porsche to school.

And yet... and yet, he has come a long way from roots in Finsbury Park's working class. He has been based in LA for the last thirty years, the same amount of time he's been married to his wife, Nora Forster, a publishing heiress from Germany. As much as he enjoys living in the United States, he is amazed at the thought of a Trump presidency. "Unfortunately, there are a lot of people out there ill-equipped to cope with what is and isn't true..."

He is firmly attached to the laws of nature.

"We know this, There are those who are scared of the future and afraid to open their minds and those who are not. On the last album there is a song called One Drop and the line is 'One Drop in all of this ocean. That's it. That's what we are. One drop and that one drop can create terrible troubles or go with the flow and the flow is the future. And you can't fight it. Otherwise, you are like King Canute with his throne on the beach telling the sea to recede so as not to get his feet wet."

He is in many ways to many people a living legend. What is that like?

"It sends a shiver up my spine. That can lead to terrible ego problems. And I'm much happier with self- doubt than self-glorification." And with that, Mr. Lydon "2016," solid citizen of suburban Malibu, says he has to go and "put up a letter box in the driveway."

ABOUT THE AUTHOR

Will Richardsson is a trained historian, writer, and TV producer. He is a pioneer in English language programming in Poland. He has produced and presented the TV shows Poland Daily Travel (travel episodes available daily since December 2018). There's a Will (a talk show first produced in Warsaw in 2019, emphasizing the Ukraine War since February 2023). Both shows are freely available on YouTube.

An inveterate traveler, he was born in North Carolina, grew up in Virginia and Georgia, studied in the USA and the UK, and lived in Los Angeles, London, Paris, Managua, and Warsaw.

Other books available on Amazon Kindle include:
Because It's There (collected published travel stories)
Roam (a satirical adventure)
That Beast Astray (a comic novel)
The Monkey Puzzle (part one of an upcoming longer work: The Scream of the Butterfly)